Magnus Edizioni, thanks the Photo Archive
of the Istituto Geografico De Agostini - Novara,
Nippon Television Network - Tokyo
and RCS Rizzoli Libri - Milan
for the kind co-operation offered in the production
of this book.

ISBN 88-7057-115-7
Printed in Italy by LitoImmagine - Rodeano Ud

ROME
a journey of dreams

Photography by
H. SIMEONE HUBER

Texts by
ARMANDO RAVAGLIOLI

Translation by
GILES WATSON

MAGNUS

Thirty glorious centuries

The overwhelming desire of anyone who has ever visited a city has always been to see it from the air. When the town lies on level ground, viewpoints can be found at the top of bell towers and on the balconies of tall buildings like cathedrals; but cities nestling beneath hills provide a special panorama. Rome lies between the two ridges of high ground that form the Tiber valley, and has always boasted a wealth of observation points from which pilgrims arriving from the north could admire the sudden appearance of the city as they came down from the Etruscan plateau.

Although nowadays one can fly everywhere, the possession of natural viewpoints is still an important feature of cities like Rome. Indeed, Rome has so many images to offer, so many astounding, fabulous sights, that it is difficult for the first-time visitor to know where to begin. Its many panoramic viewpoints give a foretaste of what is to come. Of course, artists, designers, and photographers have compiled a canon of classic panoramas too long to list, even summarily. Any visitor may note, however, how individual experience can enhance these time-honored views with the infinitely changeable conditions of light and sky at different times of day.

The overall impression of Rome from the air is that of a sea, an immense ocean of buildings which has grown over many centuries through a multitude of circumstances, changing spiritual needs, and evolving architectural styles. The cityscape is like a sea not merely in its sheer immensity as it spreads out before our eyes, but above all for the variety of this vibrant, multiform mass. Nowhere else does the panorama seem to be in such perpetual motion as in Rome, composed as it is of a wide variety of shapes, ranging from the hills where the ancient city sprang up, to the monuments that bring to life the flat space between the loops of the river, once the Campus Martius, the military parade ground.

Here in particular it seems as though the expanse of buildings flowing, lava-like down from the volcanic Alban hills, has not yet cooled and set, such is the number of cupolas bubbling up out of the tightly packed townscape.

But, whether sea or volcanic magma, Rome's immensity is firmly attached to the ground. There are no spiky Gothic landmarks or grandiose bell towers here to break up the panorama. Cupolas are redolent of organ music, mystic inspiration, and aesthetic exaltation, but belong solidly to the soil. They are symbolic of that concrete sense of reality which has characterized all the historical events and intellectual movements in the city.

We shall propose a series of preliminary images to those readers who will join us on our journey of discovery: a sequence of panoramas from various viewpoints. As well as the classic views from the Janiculum and the Pincio (from east and west, to appreciate the most significant light conditions during the day), we shall offer other views from the city center that take advantage of the natural elevations overlooking it, and shall attempt to reproduce the everyday experience of Rome's residents as they look out from their balconies to enjoy the scenery. There are Trinità dei Monti, the Quirinal Palace, the Vittoriano whose terrace enhances the already spectacular Capitol, the Aventine hill offering us a less usual view from south to north, the cupola of St. Peter's, and the panoramic terrace at the Monte Mario Observatory.

First one, then another, then yet another of the various aspects that go to make up Rome's extraordinarily complex cityscape can be appreciated in turn. There is the sumptuous Baroque city to be seen from the Pincio and Trinità dei Monti, the political city that has grown up around Montecitorio (the lower chamber of the Italian Parliament), and the more lively, popular area around the Fountain of Trevi, to be seen from the Quirinal. From the Vittoriano terrace, we may look out over an immense archaeological site and, in another direction, the 19th-century Via Nazionale and 18th-century Via del Corso resemble a relief model. From the Aventine, we can follow the Tiber's course through the city center and note the island that allowed trade to develop in early times. The Janiculum offers us views of bustling, plebeian Trastevere, with its central district set into the widest loop of the river.

The Borghi, sliced in two by the modern Via della Conciliazione right up to the majestic Castel Sant'Angelo, lies spread out before the Vatican cupola, while from the vantage point of the Astronomical Observatory, we may observe an area of recent expansion between the Via Flaminia, the Parioli, and the Tiber's sinuous curves.

Rome lies before us in all its endless variety of form, symbolism, and history, the great, many-faceted city of Rome, the Rome whose history stretches over the last 30 centuries, pagan Rome and Christian Rome, ancient Rome and modern Rome. There is a Rome for those in search of echoes of ancient glory and another for those who wish to pray and meditate. There is a Rome for those who wish to experience for themselves the romantic emotions of the great travelers of the 17th, 18th, and 19th centuries, and yet another for those who crave the quintessence of artistic creativity in the collections of fine art.

Our many-sided panorama has further aspects of Rome to reveal. *Roma italiana* is aggressively present in the excessively white bulk of the Vittoriano and the hugeness of the Palace of Justice, but is also to be found in the more picturesque and colorful image of the seat of temporal power, the Quirinal, which Popes passed on to Kings, and they to the Judiciary of the Republic.

Next, there is a *Roma universale* in a series of gigantic monuments ranging from Hadrian's Mausoleum with its guardian angel on top, put to practical use first as a fortress, then as a Renaissance residence, and now as a museum, to the massive structure of the Vatican, the most impressive construction to rise up on Roman soil over many ages of inspired building. The harmonious lines of the immense cupola by

Michelangelo seem to be mirrored in the innumerable cupolas all over the ancient Campus Martius: from those in Piazza del Popolo to the church of St. Charles'; to Jesus', St. Agnes' and St. Andrew's, to the dome of St. Luke and St. Marina on the edge of the Roman Forum, and finally to the domes of the New Church and St. John of the Florentines. The cupola of St. Ivo's is sharply whimsical and brings to mind northern Gothic. It marks the ancient chapel of La Sapienza University. The domes, whether we think of them as hillocks on a plain or bubbles in volcanic lava, would appear to end at the feet of the hills, were it not for two which stand out on the horizon framing the tallest bell tower in the city. These are the domes and bell tower of Great St. Mary's on the Esquiline.

Rooftop terraces peek out from among the domes. The towers, having been cut back for the most part, do not stand out; neither do the Romanesque bell towers, despite having been brightened up by Arab tiling and provided with two-light and three-light windows by Roman marble masons.

These terraces, symbol of the pride of the great families, represent the advent of peace as the temporal power of the Popes crushed the arrogance of the barons. As emblems of civic prosperity, they provide a nice counterpoint to the spiritual majesty of the cupolas. Apart from the viewing turret of the Quirinal, there is only one real tower to be seen on the horizon, a tower with its origins in times of war but now transformed into a symbol of civic unity, the tower of the Capitol. Two contrasting symbols brought together by history rise over it: the statue of the Goddess Rome and a huge Cross.

Other noteworthy landmarks may be picked out, such as the outline of the statues on the cathedral of St. John in Lateran, which enact the world's choice of redemption. Then there are the Apostles with Christ, the turrets of the Villa Medici and the small bell towers of the church of Trinità dei Monti, which can be picked out against the backdrop of the Pincio hill. There is also the Astronomical Observatory, with its solar tower, in what used to be the Villa dei Mellini. Monte Mario on the Janiculum stands out, as do the Lighthouse of the Italian community in Argentina and the arches of the Great Fountain of Acqua Paola together with the epic majesty of the equestrian statue of Garibaldi.

Memories and associations come rushing back to the careful, sensitive visitor who remembers a little history. Such a visitor will trace the river's serpentine path through the amorphous mass of buildings. Now that it is hemmed in by twin lines of avenues, the Tiber resembles even more closely that dazzling belt to which it was compared in the past, a belt that once girded the entire city when it all lay on the left bank of the river. Dotted here and there are the great squares, beginning with Piazza Navona, every inch of which is a monument — it is surrounded by the ancient Stadium and dominated by both the Pamphili Palace and the church dedicated to the young martyr Agnes — and ending with Piazza di Spagna with its Rococo steps climbing up the Pincio hill.

The mind's eye can follow the narrow streets through the crowded mass of buildings along ancient routes, and find there palazzos full of works of art. We might mention the wealth of knowledge contained in the Baroque libraries, the halls of public assembly rooms, the countless places of worship, the attractive displays in the shop windows, and the vivacious, colorful market in Campo de' Fiori.

The river

If you want to get to know Rome, you have to get to know the Tiber. The best vantage points for this, those worthy of a place in our imaginary album of Roman souvenirs, are at either end of the river's course through the city, beneath Castel Sant'Angelo, and at the Tiberine Island. These are at least four points that connoisseurs of Rome must tuck away in their memories as they travel along the elegant, tree-lined Lungotevere avenues, avenues designed for horse and carriage rather than for today's necessarily more hurried traffic.

The whole of the Tiber's course through the city deserves to be treated with respect because it has remained unaltered, despite proposals made repeatedly through the centuries to create a new river bed. In this sense, the Tiber is eternal Rome's most ancient relic. Its bank below the Capitol and Palatine, and lower down towards the Marmorata where the remains of the Claudian port have come to light, speaks to us eloquently of how Rome could be defended from attack, how much water she could count on, and how easily goods could be transported — all factors which contributed to the birth and growth of the city.

Similarly, the way the river hugs the central medieval and Renaissance districts illustrates the urban development of the Campus Martius over the thousand-year period when the city had only the Tiber and its water table as a source of water. Although the Tiber is neither as long as the great rivers of the world celebrated by Bernini's stupendous fountain in Piazza Navona nor does it flow with complete regularity, it is still the longest river in peninsular Italy. That the capital of the ancient world grew up on a cluster of rocky hills lapped by the great river a short distance from it's exit into the Tyrrhenian sea is a case of geopolitical predestination, rather than of mere chance. At its estuary, the Tiber boasts a natural harbor at the center of the Mediterranean basin, the "lake" sailed by the civilizations of antiquity.

From the Milvian Bridge, which still rests on the original piers from ancient republican times and over which the great roads from the north reach the left bank, to the Risorgimento Bridge, the river, although held in check by embankments, comes close to recapturing the attractiveness we can discern in old photographs. Its green banks are home to sports stadiums and the eye can wander up to the heights of Parioli on one side and Monte Mario on the other.

Halfway along, the jewel that is Villa Madama nestles in verdant surrounds. The Villa dates back to the high Renaissance, the golden days of Pope Leo X, and was designed by Raffaello. The decoration is by his school. On the very top of the hill, the last surviving cypresses from the row that used to dominate the kiln quarries underneath wave back and forth. Many poets, including Carducci and D'Annunzio, have celebrated them in song. However, the songs to remember are those of the pilgrims who saw the whole of medieval *nobilis Roma* from here and gazed on towers, brilliantly tiled bell towers and the occasional gold roof tile which, in memory of happier times, still glittered on religious buildings. Such songs earned the hill the name *mons gaudii* (Mount of Joy), a name pilgrims gave to high ground overlooking the sanctuaries that lay at the end of their journeys of penitence. The solar tower of the Astronomical Observatory still rises haughtily over the hill. Nearby, the imaginary line of the Italian meridian passes. The Observatory incorporates the villa that the nobleman, Mario Mellini, set aside for meetings with the humanists of the 14th century. Between the river and the hill (also called the Vatican Hill because the Vatican Hills stem from it), lies the sports area of the Foro Italico, a legacy of the twenty years of Fascist rule, but a worthwhile one. The Giolitti period at the turn of the century has left us a lovely district a little further on, above the Piazza d'Armi, itself dating from King Humbert's time. This area has, oddly enough, escaped development. In the mind's eye, it extends over to the left bank of the Tiber and, indeed, on the occasion of the 1911 Exhibition, Italian and foreign cultural institutions were set up there around another villa dating back to the mid-16th century. This villa is associated with the liberal, hospitable Pope Julius III. The fine Risorgimento Bridge connects the two parts of the old Exhibition; it claims to be the first of its kind in reinforced concrete.

Indeed, most of Rome's bridges date from the last century and have no great architectural merit, although they are all very picturesque. The white Duke of Aosta Bridge merits a mention here and, further downstream, the recent underground railway bridge on its highly original piers is also noteworthy. A little beyond, on the left bank, is a vast set of flights of stairs named after the flyer, De Pinedo, who came down in his "Gennariello" in the water here on his return from an aviatory exploit. It is intended, despite its poor condition, to be a memorial to the late, lamented port of Ripetta. Why did no one strenuously defend a century ago that late Baroque masterpiece in which the sumptuous style of the triumphant Counter-Reformation melted away into the grace of Rococo? It was not the only victim of the hasty decisions made by new immigrants, whom the Romans were loath to oppose for fear of being tarred with the brush of unpatriotic conservatism.

The backdrop of the steps of the old port was altered after the demolition work that brought to light the remains of the mausoleum of Augustus. The churches of St. Rocco and St. Jerome still stand, a bold marriage of Valadier in the first case with the mannerism of Sextus V's architect in the second. Where the customs house of the port once stood, there is now the lovely Ara Pacis in its linear surround, brought to light again, together with its exquisite sculptures, after having lain for centuries among the foundations of the nearby Palazzo Fiano del Corso.

On the other side of the bridge, the Prati district, traditionally known as Prati di Castello (Castle Meadows), lies before us with its gridiron street plan framing in measured calm two noteworthy pieces of architecture. One, the modern Palace of Justice, is remarkable for its questionable taste while the other is of more solemn grandeur. It was Emperor Hadrian's mausoleum, then a bulwark of Rome's defense system against the barbarian invaders and after that, part of the defenses of the Borghi and the Vatican city. Breathtaking views may be enjoyed from the bridges and embankments here, with Michelangelo's majestic dome sheltering the world, as it were, flanked by the castle and the Janiculum.

The finest ancient Roman addition to the riverscape is without doubt the Angels' Bridge, once called the Aelian Bridge (from the *nomen* of the Emperor Hadrian). The beauty of Bernini's row of statues should not tempt us to forget the grace the bridge acquires from its five original supporting arches of differing sizes and the "donkey's back" camber of the road surface. On the left bank where the old streets, once teeming with pilgrims and money changers, fan out, the Tordinona Theatre and the Palazzo Altoviti are worthy of mention. Where there is now just a tower, there was once also a *loggia,* the only one along the whole length of the Tiber's cityside bank, created by Raffaello so some privileged individual might watch the catherine wheels lighting up the Castle. On the other side is the Hospital of the Holy Spirit, the most ancient of those built for pilgrims and for abandoned babies (for unwanted newborn children were sometimes thrown into the river). Above the older and newer hospital buildings, on top of the hill, there are still some venerable cypresses among the more modern edifices where the hospital cemetery once lay.

Opposite, on the left bank, the apse and high cupola (the "half-sucked sugared almond") of St. John of the Florentines rise up where watermills stood until 1870. Further on, closer to Sextus Bridge, (Baccio Pontelli's 1475 reconstruction of a classical bridge), we find on the right Agostino Chigi's Villa, later known as the Farnesina, and the lower section of Acqua Paola. This section recycles the water that gushes forth further up from the Great Fountain, near the hilltop and the church of St. Peter's in Montorio with its famous Bramante chapel. On the left, the majestic profiles of the Falconieri and Farnese Palazzos dominate, the only ones built with such an impressive river frontage. We are now well and truly in the heart of medieval Rome.

The original Jewish Ghetto lies to our left. Before it was shut down, it was the modest district that brought forth Cola di Rienzo. Opposite, on the right, is the foreign merchants' quarter of classical times, Trastevere, split in two by a wide, modern avenue. Between the Jewish bank and the Trastevere bank, the Tiberine Island lies apparently suspended between two ancient bridges. It brims with legend and history. Gregorovius, for example, made the decision to write his famous history of medieval Rome here.

The eye is now drawn towards the Aventine and its crown of convent churches ranging from St. Sabina's, with its memories of St. Dominic Guzman, to St. Mary of the Priorate, where the Order of Malta has its monastic seat, as once did the Templars. Just below can be seen the remains of the imperial port. These bring to mind the many, tardy plans to conserve the remains that escaped the developer's pick when the embankment was built, as well as the other plans to convert the Arsenal building opposite into a Tiber Museum.

On the right bank, the enormous restored Palazzo of San Michele, which once housed hospices, bounds the area of the ancient port of Ripagrande, now long disappeared. Great ships docked here from Ostia and Fiumicino, Rome's outlets on the coast, hauled up by teams of paired oxen. Today, only two wharves tucked against the embankment remind us of the ancient bustle and tempt us to speculate about a possible return to river transport, even if only for tourism. The sea may be reached by a navigable channel in summertime.

The old Tiber still retains its charm along this stretch in the unspoiled nooks and corners, where the ghost of Aeneas walks among the seagulls.

The city walls

One of Rome's most fundamental characteristics is the continuous line, much of it still intact, of the imperial walls. Despite later alterations, especially in the monumental architecture of the city gates, the rhythm and essential nature of the walls have remained unchanged over the centuries. Serious incursions suffered over the last century have not jeopardized their basic integrity. This has been irreparably compromised only in the area where the railway lines converge on Termini station.

The Roman walls have never played an important military role. At best, they were an imposing deterrent; but we would hesitate to call them epic, like those of Troy. Anyone who wanted to get over them did so without overmuch trouble. We look on the walls rather as bearing witness to the historical solidity of the Eternal City whose outline and size they delimited even when the total city area stretched no further than from the Capitol to the landings on the Tiberine Island. At that time, like a galaxy with a dense core and a nebulous tail, Rome's greatest imperial expansion was still reflected in the shape crystallized by the Aurelian walls.

It was the ring of city walls, fanatically conserved and almost religiously venerated in the city's hard

times of decline and contraction, that kept alive dreams of glory in Rome's decadence. The walls allowed Rome to continue to breathe the air of imperial days at times when it was a city with more trees and meadows than buildings, where nature had forced her way back into the city's abandoned spaces, breaking up the monolithic grandeur of the monuments and overwhelming minor buildings. The city was still Rome, delimited by the ancient sacred *pomoerium* (walled area) whose shape was compared to a lion's during the Middle Ages, a symbolic token of predestined grandeur imprinted on the terrain. Today, when the city no longer looks from afar as if isolated like a mirage in a desert of barren countryside, the walls no longer evoke Rome's ancient splendor. They are no longer a foretaste of the marvelous sights within. Those arriving from the south along the Via Appia or from the north on the Via Flaminia used to see the walls and their towers in the distance, like a precious ring protecting the testimony of past and present magnificence.

Thus the walls defined Rome. It is true that in the city's heyday, the walls blocked the city's expansion into the countryside with the great manor estates of the senatorial class, but it is equally true that, later on, they held at bay the mortifying reality of a city reduced almost to the size of a village. The great wide circle of walls kept alive the illusion of grandeur and promised a future revival which would have seemed impossible from behind more modest defenses. Pope Paul III and Sangallo's proposal to consolidate the circle in a more modest development with a more up-to-date defensive system did not prove popular. The very difficulty of the enterprise, and the reluctance to surrender any part of Rome's ancient glory, made certain the city's physical dimensions were preserved. The idea of a city set forever at its imperial limits won the day over down-to-earth military realism.

It is only the peace to be found in the Caffarella valley that allows us to enjoy from the countryside today an emotion with an ancient flavor, that is to say, the sight of the great arc of walls from the Ardeatine rampart to the Latina Gate and beyond. From a distance, the view is suffused with the reddish brown of bricks made from the regions's volcanic soil, brought to life by the towers and gates with their Byzantine defensive structures, and crowned by a surviving ring of green rising over the walls from within.

Elsewhere, too, the arrogant advance of modern building has left the occasional gap through which the walls may be glimpsed in a reasonably broad perspective. The stretch between the Flaminian Gate, rebuilt in the 16th century, and the Byzantine-style Pincian Gate, is thus visible.

The buildings of the Villa degli Acilii, which reinforce the naturally crumbly texture of the Pincian Hill, are followed by tall ramparts dotted with high towers, now converted into studios for the art students of the French Academy. This section is also noteworthy for the legend of the "crooked wall", which fell down when Peter was crucified, and the unedifying memory of the burial in unconsecrated ground that awaited prostitutes and actors. Vegetation follows the line of the walls at this point both inside and out, helping to preserve their original aspect. The intense green of the pines and the rich color of the ancient brick-and-travertine stone walls preserve the ancient appearance intact, so that the upper part of the Via Pinciana injects a taste of unaltered ancient beauty into the life and brilliance of the Via Veneto area. This is, admittedly, nothing when compared to some of the pictures we still have of the Villa Ludovisi which, until a century ago, stood here, a masterpiece of that typically Roman admixture of classical memories and nature. Examples of this are to be found for the most part on the edge of the city where the walls encircle a deep belt of green.

In fact, the ring of walls cuts a huge area of natural beauty into two parts, one turned to face the seemingly endless countryside, the other integrated into the city either as part of the ancient heritage of parks and gardens or as nature run wild over fallen monuments of the classical past. Near the Pincian Gate, inside the wall, the niche with the bust believed to be of Belisarius evokes the memory of the Greeks' defense against the Goths of Totila in a last desperate attempt to save a city, by now stripped of all political power, from final destruction.

Just on the other side of the gap where the Porta Salaria Gate once stood, a white travertine stone block has sealed the breach near the Porta Pia Gate that, in 1870, signalled the physical arrival of the modern age in a city living off a glorious, but sterile, past. Immediately after this memorial, the Porta Pia seems to be a monument to itself, detached as it is from the line of the walls. The religious ornamentation Pope Pius IX had executed mingles in the mind with the charge of the Bersaglieri that united Italy once again with her capital city.

For a considerable distance now, the walls run through a townscape of sufficient dignity to bear comparison with the imposing ancient remains. Then, the marks left on the walls' face imply that they incorporated the older structure of Tiberius' military camp, the Praetorian Guard Barracks. After this, the walls are in bad repair from the sealed gate of the Praetorian Guard Barracks to the Via Tiburtina, where the imposing arches of the imperial aqueducts were adapted for defense. Haste to construct a shield that would deter the barbarians, who were beginning to threaten the very heart of the Empire, led to every available building that could be incorporated into the military defense system being used. A large private house employed for this purpose can be traced in outline in the wall, just before the point where the railway runs through it.

A little further on, the walls offer us one of their most impressive sights. Here, Aurelian not only incorporated more aqueducts into the walls, but also used two triumphal arches as city gates. These had themselves been made out of the supports of two watercourses placed one on top of the other. All these aqueducts remind us that this was the highest part of the city and from here, water could be directed towards both the hills and the plain.

From the Porta Maggiore Gate, the walls spread out to include the imperial Sexorium, and the perimeter wall of the military amphitheatre was incorporated into them. Its elegant arches survive and embellish the wall, albeit somewhat incongruously, given their military origins. Along the Viale Castrense to the twin St. John's and Asinaria Gates, the former a 16th-century construction, the latter from Byzantine times, there is a succession of the towers favored by 13th-century hermits for the solitude they enjoyed here on the very edge of the medieval city. The Papal residence at the Lateran Patriarchate was not enough to promote the development of this plateau, which lacked water. For almost a thousand years, the Lateran Palace was on the one hand the political and religious center of Europe and on the other, a citadel apart from the city, on the plain between the Capitol and the Tiber. The "Papal cavalcade" between St. John's and St. Peter's, repeated several times a year, continued to forge the link that bound the Papal residence to the city in a relationship of reciprocal fascination and repulsion. It ended with the temporary abandonment of Rome by the Popes, first for Viterbo, then for Avignon, bringing the city to the brink of disintegration.

From here to the southern salient of the Porta Latina and Porta San Sebastiano Gates, where the walls reach out to encompass the rich "regions" of Porta Capena and the "Public Baths" with the magnificent Thermal Baths of Caracalla, the defensive circle offers up splendid views featuring, tall, still-intact towers. The Porta Metronia Gate has plaques commemorating the restoration carried out by the newly reconstituted Senate in the 13th century while Porta Latina, long sealed but now open again, allows us a glimpse of the architectural charms of Borromini's chapel of St. John of the Oil. Finally, the ancient Porta Appia Gate, dedicated to St. Sebastian on account of the nearby catacombs bearing his name, is, with the Porta San Paolo (or Ostiense) gate just after it, the best example of the defensive system at the time of the Emperor Honorius. An inscription carved in the gate's marble jamb stone records the victory over King Robert's Angevin army in 1327. Before we reach Porta San Paolo, the walls have the Sangallo ramparts to show us as an example of Renaissance military architecture. A new wall, never built, was to have run from here to the Colonella, a second rampart Sangallo planned on the edge of the Aventine. The ancient wall carries on to the region of Ostia where it has suffered much unjustified mutilation, so much, in fact, that the Porta San Paolo complex now stands alone in the splendid isolation of its ancient solidity.

We now come to perhaps the most enchanting stretch of the city walls, backing onto the funeral pyramid of Caius Cestius and crowned by the English Cemetery, the city's Romantic corner *par excellence*. The walls now turn towards the river in a series of lovely towers. In the Middle Ages, an iron chain stretched from here to the Trastevere walls opposite to protect the city from the expected incursions of the Saracens. On the other bank, only a few stones of Aurelian's walls remain standing because it was replaced in the 17th century by the Janiculum wall, which followed a different course. Pope Urban VIII built this wall in great haste for a war that threatened but never actually took place. A sturdy construction encircling the Janiculum, it was built to withstand artillery, and found glory when the French laid siege to it in their war against the Roman Republic in 1849. Behind Villa Sciarra, high up on the hill, the wall bears the scars of cannonballs. The new Porta Aurelia-San Pancrazio replaced the older structure in 1854.

The Janiculum walls extend to the Porta Cavalleggeri Gate, where they meet the Vatican walls, built under Michelangelo's supervision in the 16th century to defend the Papal hill. The walls reach Porta Angelica beyond St. Peter's and then Castel Sant'Angelo, opening up at the so-called Porta Castello Gate. They have been shortsightedly knocked down over the past century to permit property speculation. Thus only the 9th-century Leonine wall actually goes all the way to the castle. This later, in the period of the Papal State, became a promenade from the Vatican palaces to the Mausoleum of Hadrian. It is rich in history, with probable origins in the entrenched camp of Totila. It was later reconstructed by Pope Leo III, who used Saracen prisoners as laborers.

Any visitor able to trace the route of the full circle of walls built by Aurelian, reinforced by Honorius, and completed by Belisarius, the great general, would acquire a wealth of marvelous images. Even if the 383 towers of the Gothic war period are no longer all there, the nearly 12 miles of Roman walls hold memories both moving and exciting, as well as many genuinely beautiful views. They define Rome as a frame defines a painting and have preserved the city's original identity intact over the centuries, marking out the real Rome with its tangible record of an ideal past.

The city of waters and fountains

Fountains, beyond a doubt, provide us with some of Rome's most representative images. Whether in piazzas, in noble courtyards, under famous monuments, or among archaeological remains, fountains are an essential feature of the central districts of the city and one of the most characteristic elements of its Baroque aspect.

Fountains exalt the magnificence and farsightedness of the great building Popes, who made water an *instrumentum regni* (tool of government), such was the service aqueducts and fountains rendered to the populace. Water was a propaganda tool: its limpid jets had the power to confer an image of dominance on the capital of Catholicism. Moreover, the most significant instance of the transformation of an artifact from the object of an ancient esoteric cult, in this case the cult of Isis, into an integral part of the new Christian faith, was that of a strange fountain,

the Pigna (pine cone). It once oozed water, although it has now dried up, and sits in the great niche in the courtyard of the Vatican Belvedere. For centuries, it stood in the courtyard of the Temple of Isis in the Campus Martius, where a thin veil of water ran down its scaly surface; then for hundreds of years more it was at the center of the *cantharus,* or bowl of purification, which was the focus of "Paradise", the porticoed atrium opposite St. Peter's.

Rome, hot during the summer months, shares the cult of water with peoples of other torrid climes. The ancient Romans were masters of the Mediterranean, and carried the art of building aqueducts and the joy of abundant water wherever they went. Having depended themselves on the Tiber for water supplies for many years, they began to bring water into the city through great pipes in the third century BC. As the creation of the Empire led to an abundance in Rome of goods from all parts of the globe, water was the most abundant of all, brought in through a total of over 280 miles of carefully planned conduits. We should remember that the ancient Romans progressed from disporting themselves on the waters of the river to "naumachies", stretches of water, diverted from the Tiber, that were used for games and sports. The Flavian amphitheatre itself, which served many different purposes, could be used for nautical games. Perhaps such games also took place in the Stadium of Domitian, if we are to believe the more-or-less intentional distortion, probably echoing a half-remembered tradition, that has turned the place name "platea in Agone" into "Piazza Navona".

Then came the Thermal Baths, temples dedicated to water cold, hot and lukewarm, with hydrotherapy also available. This institution centered on water was the surrogate the imperial government found for the Forum. Facile moralizing might lead us to affirm that this distraction ended up transforming the conquerors of the world, once experts in the political and legal cut and thrust of the Forum, into flabby hangers-on and the indolent parasites of a power that no longer had its roots in the citizenry. Whatever the truth of this, the new universal power and the original Roman temperament found a compromise in the Thermal Baths under the ensign of water.

The Romans suffered particularly with the downfall of the city from world power to object of conquest and depredation, as it led to the loss of their water supply. The great aqueducts dried up where once they had distributed rivers of water to the population from Porta Maggiore and the high ground. The citizenry, shocked at the miserable condition to which the city had suddenly been reduced, contracted into the Campus Martius near the banks of the Tiber. The river bank was not stable at this point and, indeed, several times a year, the river flooded over the line of defensive walls on the left bank. These walls stretched as far as the Mausoleum of Hadrian and the next salient, which rose up to the Janiculum and Porta Aurelia from the Janiculum Bridge and Porta Settimiana. We might think of the millennium from the destruction of ancient Rome to the revival of Papal Rome as a long period of waiting for the return of clear spring water. In the meantime, the populace got by with the wells sunk into the Campus Martius water table, while a special guild of "Waterers" practiced the trade of letting river water settle in cisterns and then selling it on the streets. One step up in the hierarchy were the "Vinegar-waterers" who distributed sour-tasting spring water from the Acquacetosa and other springs on the slopes of Monte Mario and the Janiculum, or which could be found in the countryside the Via Appia traversed. When the Popes returned from Avignon after the difficult conciliar period, there was great interest in the subject of water. Nicholas V persuaded a multitude of humanists to move with him from Florence to Rome, making the latter the new cultural center of the peninsula. He was also the enlightened road maker who revised the street plan in accordance with Albati's system, as well as the restorer of the Vergine Aqueduct in 1453.

At the end of the 16th century, this was to be followed by the Felice Aqueduct of Sextus V, by the Paolo Aqueduct built by Paul V at the beginning of the 17th century and finally, in 1870, by the Pio-Marcio Aqueduct of Pius IX. In fact, this was inaugurated only ten days before the breaching of Porta Pia. The Roman reign of the Popes thus began with an aqueduct and ended with the inauguration of another, which would be the last until after the Second World War.

The return of water to Rome led to the dusting off of the overblown, rhetorical appellation, *regina aquarum* (Queen of the Waters) but above all favored the creative urge of the Baroque style. The fountain took a place of honor in the creative pantheon of the great builders. Fountains became essential to the decoration of villas, where they were flanked by waterfalls, nympheums, and grottoes dripping with water as well as by fanciful games and tricks involving jets of water, all taking on an ornamental aspect in addition to their practical value.

The Popes distributed numerous fountains around the city as proof of their sensibility and munificence, while the nobles cheered the courtyards of their palazzos by installing, in a variety of more-or-less ambitious styles, nympheums. These provided ostentatious evidence of wealth and power as the availability of water, piped from public conduits, depended on a Papal benefit and was equivalent to a sizable gratuity. In this way, the populace became reacquainted with water, so much so that makeshift "naumachies", which could be arranged by blocking the drains and outlets of the fountains, were reinvented. These were the so-called "lakes", the most famous of which took place every Saturday in summer in Piazza Navona, to the delight of children and the refreshment of horses drawing noble coaches. The first public fountains were established by Pope Gregory XIII, who began by donating to the populace some drinking fountains with cursory decorations representing animals (the She-wolf Fountain in Via dei Prefetti, the Lion Fountain in Piazza San Salvatore in Lauro, and the pathetic remains of the Sow

Fountain in Via della Scrofa). After this, the new architectural feature spread like wildfire through the piazzas. Giacomo Della Porta alone is attributed with 13 still extant. He indulged himself in variations on the theme of the stalk-shaped fountain, rising from a small basin, from which a jet of water fell back into a larger basin on the ground. This might be round or of a composite shape. With the Turtle Fountain, supported by the figures of three young boys, Della Porta introduced the fountain as a sculptural, rather than an architectural, feature. Bernini was to raise this kind of fountain to a higher plane of creativity with his masterpiece, the Fountain of the Rivers in Piazza Navona. In it, the various resources of geography, sculpture and even archaeology were called into play to exalt the glory of Pope Pamphili. With no little difficulty, an obelisk was brought from the Via Appia and then erected on the rocky base that had probably graced the nearby Temple of Serapis in classical times. Later on, obelisks and other archaeological remains were to be used on a regular basis in fountains, and Bernini himself placed a somewhat shabby one on the back of the little elephant of Minerva. Private collectors of classical marble contributed ancient artifacts to the drinking fountains and nympheums in the palazzos, emphasizing the increasingly decorative function of water in architecture.

It is surprising that Francesco Borromini, a Baroque artist of unbridled imagination, should not have taken an interest in fountains. We know only that he planned to have an awe-inspiring waterfall descend on the Tiber from the loggia of Palazzo Falconieri in Via Giulia. The project was never carried out, probably because of a lack of water for the purpose. In fact, it was his rival, Bernini, a versatile artist capable of turning his hand to the theater and set design, who conceived the fountain as a work of sublime creativity, as sculpture rather than architecture. He had perhaps learned the lesson from his father. Young Gian Lorenzo had worked with his father, Pietro, on the construction of the Barcaccia Fountain in Piazza di Spagna, half realistic representation of a boat aground in a flood, half symbolic depiction of the ship of the Church, allied to the fortunes of the Sun King.

Other imaginative works, such as the Triton Fountain, Bernini's Bee Fountain, and the Moor Fountain, predate the Fountain of the Rivers. Together, they added an important new element to the townscape with meaningful, or even ravishingly beautiful, embellishments. In the space of a few decades, this imaginative aspect was to grow in importance to become an imposing scenic backdrop in the case of the Trevi Fountain. This is a scenic representation rather than a fountain (and, indeed, a more modest, but practical, tap was sited next to the fountain itself). Thanks to the whirling movement of its many cascades, the fountain seems to share the rhythmic motion of a theatrical allegory. Salvi, its creator, had absorbed all the lessons of the past, from the organ fountains (like the one at the Quirinal) to Vasanzio's whimsical creations, such as the fountains in the

Vatican gardens. The Trevi Fountain is dedicated to the Virgin Water, which sounded pretentious to Salvi's contemporaries, and seems to us to be the last imaginative seal set on the demise of Baroque art by the sophisticated hands of Baroque's heir, Rococo. This fountain is, after the Colosseum and St. Peter's, the third of Rome's great symbolic images and also the highest expression of the celebratory function of the "water display".

Monumental fountains of this kind had been introduced by Sextus V to celebrate the completion of his Felice Aqueduct, which used water from three ancient aqueducts. Although the Moses Fountain is not a success because of the clumsy execution of the central figure, it was the model for the Acqua Paola display, the Great Fountain on the Janiculum at St. Peter's in Montorio, which is repeated in a simpler form lower down at the other Great Fountain at Sextus Bridge. The most modern "water display" is an outstanding example of contemporary art, the Fountain of the Naiads in Piazza dell'Esedra, one of the most representative works of Italian Art Nouveau. It blends architectural composition, sophisticated sculptural concepts, and a vigorous water display in complete harmony.

After 1870, when construction began to take account of the need to adapt the old Rome to the functions and size required of Italy's capital city, the decorative contribution of fountains was considerable. From this point of view, the late '20s and early '30s of this century were highly positive, renewing the 16th-century work of Pope Gregory XIII. About 30 small fountains were built round Rome, all successful marriages of architectural and sculptural creativity. They all fit in perfectly with the character and history of the district they stand in. We could mention the Fountain of the Arts in Via Margutta, the Fountain of the Papal Crowns near the Vatican, the Fountain of the Cannonballs near Castel Sant'Angelo, the Fountain of the Amphoras at Testaccio, and so on.

However, in the 40-odd years following the Second World War, a period that has witnessed the chaotic growth of Rome's outer periphery and taken a utilitarian view of street furniture, it rather looks as if the creative well of fountain building has dried up. Nothing has been added to two important modern examples near the Water Company and ENI buildings in the EUR district.

History, legend, and a certain Roman tradition of folk tales are all tied to the fountains, especially the more famous ones. For example, the cannonball fired by Queen Christina of Sweden from Castel Sant'Angelo against the main gate of Villa Medici was turned into the spout of the fountain, painted by Ingres, that stands in front of the Villa. The Porters' Fountain in Via del Corso at Palazzo De Carolis probably depicts one of the 15th-century leaders of the Waterers' Guild, while wine for the populace applauding the family's guests flowed out of the Farneses' Mascherone Fountain. The ancient fountains help to remind us of the Roman passion for coolness, clarity, and timelessness, all to be found in the spectacle of flowing water.

Villas and gardens

In contrast to a complaint often made about other cities, Rome does not lack parks and gardens. The complaint can only be made about the endless new developments built without benefit of town planning or a coherent overall idea of the residents' needs. But if we look at a map, or, better still, take a panoramic view of Rome, we can see that the historic city has a wealth of parks and those special open spaces, free of encroaching buildings, that the archaeological sites provide. The upper part of the urban panorama often reveals the hills, decked with Mediterranean pines characteristic of this region, while there are quite substantial patches of green around the edges of the Papal city. Rome, like all ancient cities, had no public parks. Anyone who wanted to enjoy a walk in the open air, however, had not far to go to be "beyond the walls" or in one of those noble villas on the outskirts of the city whose owners generously opened them up to the general public.

Just as town planning lacked the concept of tree-lined boulevards, except for the odd avenue of elms in the outskirts, the idea of a public promenade was also absent. It was only imported from France at the end of the 18th century and was put into practice for the first time in the years of the Napoleonic occupation. This was when the Pincio Gardens were planned. They were to incorporate Piazza del Popolo and extend right down to the Tiber, and were completed in their present form after the restoration. However, even in the more densely built-up areas, there cannot have been a sense of oppression as all buildings, not just the palazzos, had a relatively open space to the rear. Sometimes it was used as a vegetable garden; in any case it would only contain small ancillary buildings. These were the first open spaces to succumb to the frenzy of speculative building that followed the race to house the new capital's immigrants. Only the palazzos built on the outskirts of the city enjoyed more open space around them, such as those on the slopes of the Quirinal (Palazzo Colonna and the Colonna Gardens) and of the Janiculum (Palazzo Riario-Corsini and Palazzo Salviati). The idea of living near the city in a residence with a park or garden crystallized in the design of the 16th-century villas, inspired by the Florentine villa. Some real jewels of this kind sprang up around the city, such as Villa Madama, today called Villa Lante, the Farnesina Villa, Villa Ricci (which became Villa Medici), Villa Giulia, and also Villa d'Este on the Quirinal. This last attracted the Popes' attention, and they came to transform Villa d'Este into their other Palace, the Quirinal Palace, with an extensive garden.

Using the hinterland of the Esquiline and Viminal, furnished by Sextus V with water and roads, the Baroque centuries' sumptuous life-style led to the reclaiming of the parklands around the city walls. This had to a large extent been left to run wild, or used for cultivation of crops, and had taken over that part of the imperial city that was left to its own devices when the aqueducts were cut off. Gardens were laid out, parks established, and residences for both entertaining and pleasure were built. Where the area inside the walls was insufficient for the territorial ambitions of the householder, the zone immediately without the walls was also used. It was in this way that the green belt of parkland that encompassed the city, especially to the northeast, up until the last decades of the 19th century came into being. It was conceived on a grand scale, and maintained a fine balance between the beauty of the buildings and the landscaping of the parks.

The estates of noblemen and cardinals were so near to the city that they gave it a special flavor, with wealth and beauty jostling shoulder to shoulder with crowded districts and the abandoned, uncultivated countryside. This exciting aspect of the city was celebrated by travelers, who found nothing to compare in any other European capital. A privileged oasis of the kind could only be preserved while the demographic, social and economic balance of the city remained constant. The 19th century profoundly altered these. The erosion of the great family fortunes in the wake of the French Revolution, the arrival of the railway on the edge of the city and, finally, the need to build new residential districts for the new capital of Italy all led to the gradual abandonment of the great estates. This, in turn, led to the disappearance of large sectors of the belt of woodland, the breaking up of the green belt into a series of fragmented sections surrounded by built-up areas. Despite our chagrin at the loss of an unrepeatable spectacle and the disappearance of a typically Roman phenomenon, we must acknowledge that generation's skill at limiting the damage. The long, drawn-out legal wrangle to save Villa Borghese, and the acquisition of Villa Corsini, whose park on a vast area of the slopes of the Janiculum gave the University a botanical garden and the city a public promenade, are ample evidence of this skill. The promenade was named after Queen Margherita; it is now called the Janiculum Promenade. It faces towards the Pincio Gardens on the other side of the city.

The loss of the great villas, in particular the utterly unjustified destruction of Villa Ludovisi with its blend of landscaping and ancient remains, led to the creation, over ten years, of the Archaeological Promenade. It grew out of the idea of reclaiming and preserving ancient monuments while at the same time providing the city with a marvelous parkland that would constitute an important feature of the new Rome. Ancient glories and exceptional landscapes were to enhance the differences in elevation and rich natural vegetation. A bold policy of compulsory purchase followed. Digs in the Forums and on the Palatine, plus landscaping work, created a huge area that starts at the Capitol, reaches the Porta San Sebastiano Gate, and spreads out to the Colle Oppio Park, to the exclusive atmosphere of the Caelian Hill, to the Circus Maximus depression, and to the mystic silences of the Aventine heights. The extraordinary size of this archaeological zone in the heart of the city should not make us forget other important complexes with significant archaeological remains lying in parkland such as Castel Sant'Angelo, built on the bastions and ditches of the ancient defenses, the Savello Park on the Aventine, and the Scipios' Park. The sometimes romantic, sometimes epic images these areas leave with the visitor are probably the nearest we come to the images that fascinated the travelers of the past, mingling as they do the strength of classical building with a vigorous natural environment.

These are also the prevalent sensations to be experienced at the surviving aristocratic villas, many of which are public. In them, nature's lead is followed by history and this, in turn, by art. We find evidence of historic events, unexpected survivals from the past and marvels of landscape gardening. This is the special feature of Rome's "green" — it is a "historic green" and, at the same time, a "panoramic green" in many of the surviving villas that dominate the city from on high.

Villa Borghese is an essential part of Rome's heritage of parks. For many years, its 190 acres comprised the largest area of green space in the city and, today, it is second only to the almost 450 acres of Villa Pamphili. Villa Borghese's main virtue is, together with its eye-catching variations in level, its dynamic, ever-changing parkscape where meadow follows pine grove, hidden garden leads to lake, and the exotic perfume of the trees takes us out into the space reserved for spectacles (the Piazza di Siena) and the riding track. Scenically placed artificial ruins in the Romantic tradition echo the modest buildings dotted among the huge open spaces, the fountains in a variety of styles, and the monuments to famous people. Unfortunately, the archaeological remains and sculptures which could once be entrusted to the good sense of the visiting public are nowadays mercilessly mutilated or stolen. The Villa's ancient trees are also under threat from automobile pollution. The trees have to be replaced gradually, with great care, to avoid jeopardizing this important part of Rome's heritage. The jewel in the crown of Villa Borghese is the ancient pleasure lodge, housing an exclusive collection of works of art from the Borghese family's palazzo in the city. The collection is primarily of paintings; it replaced the exceptional collection of sculpture which was transferred to the Louvre under Napoleon.

Villa Celimontana also lies in the middle of an area of great historical and archaeological interest, with the Claudianum's evocation of imperial Rome, the churches of St. Gregory's and Saints John and Paul from the early centuries of Christendom, and the medieval monastery of the Four Sainted Kings. The Villa seems to echo with the sounds of the edifying entertainments staged here in impromptu fashion by St. Philip Neri, halfway around the penitential pilgrimage of the Seven Churches.

Villa Sciarra, on the slopes of the Janiculum, retains vestiges of the imperial walls and, on its own 17th-century walls, the marks of the epic story of 1849. One is compelled to ask when better standards of public behavior will make it possible for its famous

peacocks to wander the gardens undisturbed.
Villa Doria-Pamphili, the city's largest parkland acquisition in recent decades, suffered great damage as a result of the Via Olimpia slicing through, although this could be remedied in part by a few footbridges. The Villa is intimately linked to the Garibaldian adventure and preserves splendid corners of natural beauty. However, constant maintenance is necessary for the water displays, the flower beds, and other ornamental details. The nearby catacombs add to the Villa's fascination.

Villa Mellini, on top of Monte Mario with its main building converted into an Observatory, offers us, apart from an incomparable view over the dome of St. Peter's, the memory of famous guests, including Goethe.

Villa Torlonia has also been reclaimed recently, being in a serious state of disrepair because of the authorities' scandalous indulgence of the vandalism perpetrated by the villa's visitors. It boasts a varied sample of those facilities required to entertain in what was almost a princely court. A *nouveau riche*, newly ennobled individual like Torlonia had to concentrate everything in a limited area.

We should also mention the Valle Giulia's wide range of panoramic views. It is a large zone of building development discreetly set in parkland, the buildings all related to cultural life. There is still an air of the educated hospitality that originally inspired Pope Julius' cultured, humanistic Villa.

Neither should we forget the open spaces of the new EUR quarter, where the lake with its illuminated fountain is one of the few non-utilitarian items built after the war. The 19th-century gardens in the middle of new squares like Piazza Cavour and Piazza Vittorio Emanuele are also of interest. The latter is awaiting renovation after the ravages left by a street market held there.

Other noteworthy green spaces in the city are some of the great tree-lined avenues like Viale Mazzini, between the Risorgimento Bridge and Piazzale Clodio below Monte Mario. Its has a long central section is landscaped with oaks and box trees. Others are Viale delle Milizie and Viale Giulio Cesare in Prati, Viale Regina Margherita in Parioli, Via Nomentana sedately strolling between rows of sophisticated houses, or the Lungotevere avenues themselves. Plane trees set a keynote everywhere.

The visitor can also find experiences and impressions of Rome in other more modern parks like the one laid out up at Villa Glori (more of a vineyard than a noble villa) with its memories of patriotic derring-do. The small pine grove of Monte Sacro should not be overlooked. It contains the classical Aviene bridge. Then there is the Testaccio park, next to the cemetery by the walls, which also bears witness to some foreigners' links with Rome.

The lover of Rome, however, is always thinking about the long-awaited, much-hoped-for, yet-to-be-completed archaeological park on the Via Appia. A decision must be made to set it up, both to comply with the town plan and to redeem the generation that sacrificed the incomparable Roman countryside, a "historic countryside" worthy of its "historic center", to the greed of developers of the most abject kind. One day, this will be the most authentically Roman park. It will be a destination not only for excursions into a natural environment, but also for trips across time, as one strolls along the ancient pavements or over meadows dotted with the graves and villas of classical senators, or descends into the catacombs where the early Christians wrought their long, patient revolution. When the park is built, Rome will have received recompense from our generation with its throwaway culture. Rome is too full of significance to be truly understood by a consumer society such as ours.

The fascination of the past

Other cities with as illustrious a history and civilization as Rome — Athens springs to mind — attract visitors to their fabulous archaeological remains and impressive monuments, but no other city possesses the sheer wealth of ancient monuments to be found in Rome. This is understandable if we take into account the fact that no other center of the ancient world achieved the size and wealth of Rome, nor did any other city survive the centuries with its sense of worldwide importance intact.

In every age, her praises have been sung. This eternal admiration reached a peak in the Middle Ages, when Europe began to shake off the heavy chains of the Dark Ages and looked to Rome as an impossibly perfect model to be emulated. Rome's *mirabilia* (wonders) prompted pilgrims who arrived in search of indulgences to explore the city's streets, where collapsing buildings were as regular a feature as the monumental remains of the past. Moreover, at that time, there were many more monuments than there are today.

However much marble and metal the scavengers removed (incidentally contributing raw materials to Rome's meager export trade), the imperial palaces, the thermal baths, the basilicas, and the temples still seemed very much part of an integrated whole. Only the Renaissance and the building fever of the Popes would deplete Rome's archaeological reserves to any significant extent.

The pilgrims' appreciation would be echoed, later in Europe's history, by the admiration of the artists who came to immerse themselves in classicism, and by the scions of the emerging commercial, pre-industrial middle class who arrived on their Grand Tour. At that time, "ruinism" actually became an artistic category, in demonstration of the depth of sentiment the ancient glories excited in the viewer's soul. Visitors gazed open-mouthed at the huge buildings, which were without rival among contemporary structures in their own countries. There were remains of uncertain origin, with all sorts of folktales attached to them, dotted around the abandoned areas of the city.

In the districts that were still inhabited, the remains were only partially on view, and were often distorted.

They became buried deeper and deeper by the progressive elevation of the ground level, as well as by often-vulgar, arbitrary accretions adapting them to other purposes in a wild confusion of the ancient and the modern.

Astonished pilgrims went from the relics of classical beauty to the most squalid misery of the time. Rome's hold over foreign visitors was strong. The sight of past greatness, swarming with people in a process of almost biological decomposition as the poor sought a means of survival, was a powerful one. Above this atmosphere of disintegration rose the new ecclesiastical buildings, their huge domes and daring architecture challenging the past in a stunning contrast. Is not this the little Roman world Pinelli's joyful watercolors celebrate, as much as Roesler Franz's decadent canvasses?

When the rough-and-ready search for antiquities slowly turned into scientific archaeology, the process of separating the heritage of the past from the everyday life of the city began. At the end of the 18th century, the Romans began to move from their houses near the walls, which had been built over ancient remains. Archaeologists brought the remains of still more ancient monuments to light, together with clues that enabled them to reconstruct the city's classical development. The phenomenon is graphically demonstrated in Campo Vaccino, a regular square surrounded by modern buildings, churches built over important classical remains, and the perimeter wall of the Farnese Gardens on the Palatine. There is a drinking trough in the middle of the square, standing under the columns of the Temple of the Dioscuri: a sign that livestock were brought to market here. There used to be a strange mixture of the past, more hinted-at than stated in the trappings of greatness, and the routine world of everyday cares.

Today the same area, with the surviving churches looking down on it, presents us with a vast area of ancient ruins chopped off just above ground level. We can see that the dignified city that had its principal cattle market here is dead and gone. It was inevitable that, given civilization's obsession with enlightenment and the sciences, the *de facto* juxtapositions arising over the centuries around the ancient remains should be rejected, despite the emotional force they derived from the vitality of the present and the weight of the past.

The Palatine remains were methodically excavated, and a beautiful garden was sacrificed in the process. In more recent times, and pursuing a similar line of thought, the Auditorium of the Augusteum would be destroyed in the search for the bare, breached, surviving walls of Augustus' Mausoleum. There is no way of reconciling the aesthete's regrets with a researcher's curiosity, and the victory of curiosity has freed us from an over-Romantic vision, created over the centuries, that does not correspond to the reality of any historical period. It has been a process of dissection, or "deconstruction", so to speak.

The dead city of the Forums or the Imperial Palaces of the Palatine give a rather different prospect from that which past visitors saw. They show a dimension of the ancient past that would perhaps be incomprehensible to the great panoramic artists and the early photographers. They have left us incomparably beautiful images of that state of "life in the midst of death" that was to be found in these areas. It must, however, also be recognized that the unadulterated archaeological view highlights the greatness, the severe majesty of the ruins as the surrounding stillness emphasizes their empty perspectives and silent spaces. The core of the classical city's surviving remains is to be found between the Capitol and the Colosseum, the Domus Augustana and the Domus Aurea, and the Forum Romanum and the Fora Imperialia. The Colosseum; the three triumphal arches of Titus, Septimius Severus, and Constantine; Trajan's Column; the Basilica of Massentius; the remaining columns of the great temples; and the Tabularium providing a sub-structure for the modern Capitol Palazzo; all help to recreate the matchless glory of the past.

It is a glory that becomes majesty when we think of how a small town came to unify the known world, and at the height of its powers and wealth received tributes of raw materials and works of art from every corner of that world. From being a town of brick and wood it turned into a city of rare marble, enhanced by the labor and creativity of people of all races with obelisks, columns, bronze statues, and the exotic articles on show under the porticoes of the Imperial Forums, in the entrance halls of temples, or in the collections of patrician residences.

The visitor to Rome will at first be confused by such a wealth of allusion. It will all seem like so many messages from outer space. Examining the surviving remains of everyday life in classical times is likely to be an easier task. Among such articles we could mention the game of nine mens' morris on the floor of the Julian Basilica, the marks of the money changers' coins melted by fire on the floor of the Emilian Basilica, and the Tullian Prison, where those great enemies of Rome, Jugurtha, and Vercingetorix were certainly imprisoned, even if the apostles Peter and Paul may not have been, despite the tradition to the contrary. There are the churches established in the Temple of Antoninus and Faustina (St. Laurence in Miranda) and in the Temple of the Goddess Rome (New St. Mary's or St. Frances the Roman), in the hall of the Temple of Peace (St. Cosmas and St. Damian), and in the Imperial Library (St. Mary the Liberator). It is impossible to list the remains in the archaeological zone *par excellence,* which extends to the main thermal baths, or, indeed, to evoke the range of emotions their contemplation excites. The visitor should not hurry. The experience should be sipped like wine, impressions noted, and a second visit planned, perhaps another time, to gain a complete idea of Rome. In ancient times, visitors stayed for a whole season.

In the central districts there are other ancient remains everywhere. They produce a different reaction, as ancient styles stand shoulder-to-shoulder with more recent ones. This is the case with the Pantheon, the best preserved ancient monument. It is the case with Marcus Aurelius' column, the Egyptian obelisks, and the Thermal Baths of Diocletian. It is difficult to collect and order in the mind all these impressions and experiences, to which we should add those engendered by the monuments and spaces from subsequent stages in Rome's development.

We would like the visitor to dedicate special attention to classical Rome as it appears in the context of more recent construction, or as it can be seen through the lines of later buildings. We suggest a walk around the Theater of Pompey, whose auditorium, especially, is recognizable in outline, its horseshoe shape reproduced in the line of palazzos in Piazza dei Satiri. We must also mention here the ring of buildings round Piazza Navona, superimposed upon the terraces of the Stadium of Domitian. Impressive remains of the stadium have been found as much as 20 feet below present ground level. This was the ground level in ancient times. The remains can be best observed at the northern curve of the square. Other ancient remains have come to light in the excavations in the middle of Largo Argentina, and in the deep excavation in the Piazza Sallustio.

We wish, at this point, to refer to the archaeological finds in various parts of the city, above all to the remains of Nero's Domus Aurea, buried under the foundations of the Thermal Baths of Trajan and later treated as a "grotto" by the artists in Raffaello's circle. After its discovery, it was here that the artists of the Renaissance learnt the art of stucco and "grotesque" decoration. There are also important remains undergound in many churches, particularly St. Clement's, which has three levels. On these levels, we find ancient Roman buildings of different periods, and occasional Mithraeums, places of worship dedicated to the Oriental religion which competed with early Christianity. The underground remains of the house where the basilica of St. John and St. Paul now stands are very interesting, as are those of the house under the basilica of St. Cecilia, in Trastevere. We may also view Augustus' Ara Pacis, brought to light from the foundations of Palazzo Fiano on the Corso, now that it has been placed in front of the Emperor's Mausoleum. Its well-preserved sculptures remind us of the archaeological treasures that may still lie buried under the city, and that folktales claim can still be found in the bed of the Tiber, for this has also risen over the centuries.

Whatever the truth of the matter, the ethereal Loggia dei Cavalieri opened during the Renaissance over the walls of the Forum of Augustus may be considered an eloquent symbol of this stratification and the continual re-elaboration of the same basic raw material throughout the city.

The rediscovery of far-off periods of Roman life under more recent buildings, themselves later converted as the needs of the state and the dictates of fashion changed, is one of the most profound experiences Rome can offer the visitor. For example, if we take the obelisk in Piazza Monticitorio, we should remember that it came to light only 200 years ago, having lain undergound for over a thousand years. Behind the church of St. Laurence in Lucina and under the basements of some of the buildings in Via di Campo Marzio, work is still going on to bring to light the table with the hour-markings of the sundial for which the obelisk was the *gnomon,* or indicator. When one remembers one is walking over layers of the city's history, with the prospect of new finds by archaeologists always possible, the visit to Rome becomes an adventure as well as a discovery.

From primitive christianity to the middle ages

A thousand years separate the glory of Imperial Rome from what is called the Rome of the Papacy, exuberant and sumptuous in its Baroque style. This style developed architectural motifs that had already been present in the decorative elements of Imperial Rome. We can trace the course Rome took from the first period to the second, as the city's institutions broke down, and habits and ideals changed. The change is visible not only in the stones, but also in the attitudes of the people and the function of the city. An ideal heritage from the past combined with new impulses producing conflict, torment, and humiliation. Above all, there was a profound restructuring of the civic values Rome had inherited from its imperial past.

It is quite amazing to find over this long arc of time that Rome preserved, to the point of paradox, its self-image even in the worst of times. Rome was convinced that she was "different" and had a special role to play, that of symbolizing the civilized ideal of the world, of safeguarding the principle of political unity, of being the foundation of a universal empire. This deeply felt conviction emerged in the darkest of hours, sometimes as veneration of ancient ruins, sometimes as the claim to the right to assign the crown of the Holy Roman Empire and the office of Pope. Rome spent centuries in a kind of coma, unable to adapt to the realities of politics and religion that, while beyond Rome's grasp, sought legitimacy on Roman soil in front of Rome's imposing ancient remains. Finally, after many tribulations, as temporal power passed to holders of other prerogatives, Rome found internal peace again with the Papacy and a renewed culture, a synthesis of all the city's classical and Christian experience.

This millennium of turmoil and revolution left its mark on the city, notwithstanding the changes that have often moved the city's center of gravity, notwithstanding the external transfiguration of the Baroque period, and notwithstanding much demolition over the last hundred years. Dark-Age Rome has left its unmistakable mark in the splendid basilicas of the post-Constantine era, when art and culture were slow to adapt to the political and social degradation of the city; in the austere Romanesque churches bearing the mark of Byzantine rule; and in the various reconstructions that followed each other in the periods of cultural renewal, like the Carolingian era and that of the resurgence of the Communes. Furthermore, there are the surviving towers, which tell of factions among the citizenry unable to identify either with the Pope or with the free regiment of the Commune. Last of all, there is the urban fabric, still twisting through the quarters that grew up among the rubble of the ancient city's dissolution. It has the same shape and character as ever, despite the changes wrought by the different styles of the buildings to be found there.

The early Christian basilicas are the link between classical Rome and the resurgent grandeur of Baroque Rome. Throughout the centuries witnessing the slow collapse of neglected ancient buildings — now *res nullius* despite attempts at restoration from the time of Theodoric to the Byzantine Dukes and the Emperors of the family of the Othos — the Christian basilicas, which echoed the glory of the civic basilicas, were preserved and decorated with mosaics and paintings. Although we look at them through a filter of structural alteration and elaboration, the few patriarchal basilicas and some other churches, notably St. Mary in Trastevere, take us back to the time when, with the seat of Empire now in the East, all Rome's pretentions to greatness had to fall back on ecclesiastical arguments.

In particular, Great St. Mary's, even with its Baroque additions of the two side chapels, facade and some later mosaic decorations, is still the best example of the city's surviving capacity for grandeur at the end of the classical period. The language of the mosaics of Great St. Mary's speaks both of surviving artistic abilities in the fifth century (the decoration of the triumphal arch and the wall scenes) and of the 13th-century renewal (the apse and facade). No other Roman monument is so complete a witness to evolution through stages in the history of art.

Different moments in the long Dark Ages are represented by various churches, oases of splendor in the desert of those difficult times. They often arose where ancient buildings had stood, replacing perhaps small public baths or military billets, or else they were adapted from the private chapels of large houses. Many used all sorts of looted material, and are sometimes a palimpsest of restructuring and decorative additions. The following are essential to a complete knowledge of the city: St. Praxedes'; St. Clement's, on the wide road to St. John's (the descent to the lower levels is not to be missed); the church of the Four Sainted Kings; St. Stephen the Round, a unique example of a building with esoteric symbolic significance; the Capitoline church of the Aracoeli; the church of St. Cosmas and St. Damian in the Forum; the group of churches of the Greek Bank, which commemorates the Byzantine dominium of the eighth century; St. Mary in Cosmedin; St. George in Velabro; St. Theodore's; St. Nicholas-in-the-prison; and so on. Outside the walls, to "see" the Dark Age Roman Church, one cannot miss St. Laurence in Verano and St. Agnes', the latter with the Mausoleum of Constance next door and its bright mosaics of unusual Bacchic scenes.

Christian art of the period features mosaics frequently. It is difficult to understand why the so-called Dark Ages, which were, indeed, a period of general civil regression darkened by many barbaric acts and much human suffering, should find expression at Rome in an art characterized by light and splendor, not just in gold, but in all the colors of the rainbow. While other arts related to building languished and died, the Oriental art of mosaic took such hold in Rome that at every period of civil and cultural renewal, however relative, it surged ahead. Rome is comparable to Ravenna and Venice for mosaics, both in quantity and artistic importance. But it is unique for the length of the period over which this form of artistic expression extends, from the sixth century to the ninth, tenth and 13th when even Giotto used it, and beyond. For nearly a thousand years, the art of mosaic cast a shaft of light over the Dark Ages.

There is a long series of mosaic masterpieces — apart from the Esquiline, Lateran, and Ostian basilicas — including the churches of St. Cosmas and St. Damian, St. Pudentiana, St. Praxedes, St. Theodore, St. Laurence and St. Agnes (both basilicas outside the walls), St. Cecilia, St. Mark, St. Mary in Domnica, St. Clement, New St. Mary, St. Mary in Trastevere. The list is endless.

As well as the mosaics and related works of art, we may admire the surviving creations of the Roman marble masons. This craft is unique to Rome because of the limitless availability of marble from ancient monuments in disrepair. Using these remains, the marble masons and their splendid, energetic creations were forerunners of the artistic revival of the city. Repaving the floors of the great basilicas might be thought of as mosaic on a grand scale. These ancient surfaces were relaid with a richer range of materials and an artistic sensibility influenced by Arab decorative art. By matching the fragments of marble of different colors and qualities to be found near at hand, the marble masons were able to carpet the floors of the basilicas with eye-catching displays. We find the most successful of these in St. Mary in Trastevere and at St. Chrysogonus', where the paving has obviously also inspired the multi-colored panelled ceilings added in the 16th century. The marble masons also used more massive blocks, saved from the lime kilns, to make elegant spiral columns with subtle veins of mosaic for the *tympanum* tabernacles, the great chandeliers, the cloisters, and for a new kind of sepulcher where inlaid marble was juxtaposed with mosaic.

The cloisters the marble masons built are the best places to appreciate the atmosphere of the decaying metropolis in the Dark Ages, and of solitude in a place once thronging with people. The atmosphere can be felt most keenly in the cloister of St. John in Lateran and in the Four Sainted Kings of St. Paul outside the walls.

Other areas of silence are the great open spaces on the hills that the built-up parts of the city have isolated, the Aventine and the Caelian. These therefore stand as special examples of the remote past. In the 16th century, the poor state of repair of so many of the monuments and other architectural complexes combined with a change of taste and the activism of a period of revival, and led to the demolition of many of medieval Rome's most important buildings.

The most serious loss was without doubt that of the Lateran Patriarchate, which had been the lodestar of the Universal Church for ten centuries. The demolition decreed by Sextus V did, however, spare its most moving aspect, that of the supreme manifestation of the cult of holy relics, a cult that brought millions of pilgrims to Rome and led to the institution of the Jubilee. The Sancta Sanctorum (Holy of Holies), with the Holy Steps leading up to it, is a living fragment of medieval Rome flanked by many, often stylistically doubtful, resting places of relics. Among these is the nearby church of the Holy Cross of Jerusalem, into whose crypt the earth of the Mount of Olives was poured, and which holds the most important splinter of the wood of the Cross, recovered by St. Helen, mother of St. Constantine.

One of the best preserved medieval centers is the Tiberine Island, if we except the modern hospital although even this also maintains the ancient tradition of the island sacred to Aesculapius. From the Matilda Tower to the convent and the church of St. Bartholomew, everything is firmly rooted in the period around the year 1000 AD and seems to breathe the atmosphere of the Othos and the times when they were trying to re-establish the seat of empire. Passing over to the left bank of the river, where the old Ghetto was hastily knocked down, there are other signs of the early Middle Ages, especially at the church of St. Angelo, built from the remains of Octavia's Portico, and in some of the houses near the Theater of Marcellus. This has been freed of the medieval accretions to its lower arches, but still shows traces of the alterations all the major monuments suffered when they became the main economic resource of the population. The Romans exploited their abundant heritage of ancient buildings and, indeed, were unable to explain their existence at all except in terms of legend and folktale. A huge tract of the Middle Ages disappeared with the demolition of Piazza Montanara and the zone corresponding to what is now Via del Teatro di Marcello. But an immense block still displays the features of the Middle Ages in Via del Portico d'Ottavia, Via delle Botteghe Oscure, and Piazza Margana, or in other central areas like Campo de' Fiori, Piazza Navona, and the Pantheon, down to the roads along the Tiber (like Via Monte Brianzo) where the pilgrims lodged. We find more little centers of a clearly medieval nature in Trastevere, in Suburra, around Great St. Mary's, and on the great road of St. John's going up to the Lateran Palace.

A quarrelsome, noisy medieval route could be traced through the central districts, going from tower to tower — from the more obvious examples, to those partly knocked down and incorporated into later buildings, coming finally to those converted into roof terraces on the princely palazzos of more opulent days. Since the ground between the Imperial Forums and the Papal seat at the Lateran Palace was the favorite battleground of popular armies and the troops of Popes and Emperors, it is here that we find some of the most imposing towers: the Torre delle Milizie, the Torre dei Conti, the Torre degli Annibaldi, the Torre del Grillo, the present-day bell tower of St. Francis of Paola at St. Peter-in-chains, the tower of the Four Sainted Kings, the Capocci towers at St. Martin-in-the-mountains, and so on.

Another possible route might go past where the lime kilns burned near the great monuments, to show how the in the hardest centuries of her history, Rome survived by reducing ancient remains to lime and even by exporting her precious marble. One need only remember that the Lateran hospital existed thanks to the use of one third of the Colosseum as a quarry, and that the Hospital of the Consolation sold every last column and cincture of the Julian Basilica.

These are examples of what we might call institutionalized vandalism. The vandalism of the thousands of individual despoilers, however, was even more instrumental in removing, wholly or in part, so many mementoes of past glory. Scavengers took everything there was to take of the remains they had outside their doors, breaking them up, destroying them, and using them as objects of barter in a systematic, day-by-day despoliation that resembled professional burglary. Folktales grew up around casual discoveries of little treasure troves, and led to rumors of fabulous riches still waiting to be dug up from the ground under the city.

All in all, this mysterious, turbulent millennium fills a place in the Roman imagination as important as that occupied by more sensational times. Dark Age Rome's profile can be clearly seen in the city's topography, its language can be heard in the place names, and its art can be seen all around.

Rome triumphant

The return of the Popes from Avignon rapidly stimulated the city to become a symbolic metropolis, not only because of its historical and religious significance, but also because of its majestic townscape. In a few short decades, an extraordinary urban renewal took place thanks to the rivalry of Popes and religious orders, cardinals and guilds, creating a spectacular new look for the languishing city. This renewal was not, of course, a result of a new economic boom or a resurgence of civic pride. Poverty and a subsistence economy, hinging on agriculture and, to a lesser extent, on crafts and commerce, were still the order of the day. Rome nevertheless became majestic once again, an object of renewed admiration, just as she surrendered her independence, acknowledging the great vitality and renewed glory she drew from her symbiotic relationship with the Papacy.

Naturally, the Popes were motivated to restructure the town plan by the same drive other new sovereigns felt at that time to shape their capitals. The royal center was to be a worthy setting for political and administrative activities and was to enhance the court's splendor. The Popes, the new absolute rulers of the Papal State being formed on the foundations of the ancient Estate of St. Peter, felt a need to surround their dual role of temporal rulers and heads of Christendom with glory. Rome was no longer an ordinary city but the source of *magisterum* (doctrine) and influence and had to display, in a renewed external majesty synthesizing past and present, both the creative force of a faith preaching the exaltation of man through adoration of the godhead and the ecclesiastical organizational ability to maintain unity throughout the world.

New, straight roads took the place of the tortuous paths that had sprung up higgledy-piggledy over the preceding centuries. Places of pilgrimage began to look richer as a result of believers' gifts. The major churches, slowly imitated by lesser places of worship, acquired domes; the palazzos decorated with stuccoes and frescoes took on new dimensions. In general, Rome became a show city, designed to involve visitors, not so much in trade or exchange or the emulation of these works, as in the liturgy of the sumptuous religious ceremonies, the theatrically produced processions, and the rituals of the Jubilee. Rome thus reacquired her fame, and a journey to Rome became a *sine qua non* even after much of Europe had thrown off the influence of Roman Catholicism.

Two types of renewal carried out by the Popes are of paramount importance: the hagiographic and the symbolic, in Piazza San Pietro (St. Peter's Square) and Piazza del Campidoglio (Capitol Square), respectively. The long period of gestation required for the reconstruction of St. Peter's delayed the creation of its gigantic square until well into the Baroque period, but its eventual execution was implicit right from the first hammer blow Bramante gave to the structure of Constantine's days, which had to be removed to make way for the more grandiose construction. Such an edifice had to have an immense entry area where the pilgrims would congregate.

The Capitol, renovated by Michelangelo, received a symbolic forum where welcoming and reception were the keynotes. The Capitol Square, Piazza del Campidoglio, was open like a stage on the side facing the city, and was an object of admiration for those drawn from afar by the magic of the name, Rome. The square is not large; it centers on a statue gesticulating in a manner at once imperious and pacific. It has a power of attraction that the market place that once stood in front of the Capitol building did not.

It was Paul III's inspiration to exalt the legal and political tradition of Rome as a complement to the universal rule of the Church. This exaltation of antiquity, which the popular Commune could not take past the stage of Cola di Rienzo's rantings, became a serious subject for apologetics in the hands of the Popes. The appeal of the two poles of Roman life — St. Peter's and the Capitol — blended together and would counterbalance each other in the future, particularly after the completion of Bernini's huge portico in the Vatican. This synthesis of the secular and the divine was to make up the characteristic message of the Papacy and the city that is its home.

Rome's renewal in the period from the 15th to the 18th centuries was such a powerful stimulus that all the great capitals of the world were to copy its forms with huge domes, long straight avenues, fountains bubbling in the squares, and luxurious settings for noble palazzos. Michelangelo, Vignola, Borromini, and Bernini furnished the models for building and decoration to a world community that continued to hold unity of form paramount, even when that unity was rather less than complete.

The city's renovatory drive lasted for centuries before exhausting itself on the eve of the events involving Rome in the unification of the Italian peninsula, a process with European implications. In the end, the restructuring absorbed the remaining urban and monumental aspects from other eras.

Although medieval Rome was not overwhelmed or vitiated stylistically by the Baroque additions, it became incorporated into the overall picture presented by the dominant newer buildings. For this reason, Rome's Renaissance-Baroque side is prevalent over all the others and is the most complete expression of the city's character. No one would use a Renaissance bell tower to symbolize Rome, or a picturesque Trastevere back street. Everyone thinks of domes and fountains, statues declaiming in the squares, and the winged figure of Fame on palazzo facades.

Surprisingly, the stylistic and creative contributions of different centuries manage to coexist in harmony. Baroque decoration and even the rather affected ostentation of its final form, Rococo, prove to be functions of the same artistic logic, the same art of rendering architecture majestic by enriching it with layers of allusion.

The figurative arts worked hand in hand to achieve this aim of exaltation, producing immense cycles of work, enormous compositions in the vaults and domes, while skilled craftsmen furnished the accessories and decorations to blend into the spirit of the architecture. This "Rome Triumphant" still greets the visitor and is never out of sight. It will go with the visitor to the great monuments, it will be the culmination of the city's many layers, it will form a background to the city's medieval aspects, it will encompass all the fountains and characterize the great parks. In the end, columns, arches, vaults, domes, fountains, and villas will remain in the visitor's visual memory and become the essence of Rome.

Let us take a look at the streets and squares. The most typical streets, Renaissance from the town-planning point of view but often lined with Baroque buildings, are the great, long, straight avenues designed by the architects of the Rinascimento. Even Raffaello was, in this sense, an architect as he laid out Via Ripetta. Via Giulia, Via Condotti, and Via del Governo Vecchio are the best examples of 16th-century streets. The so-called Trident, extending from Piazza del Popolo, exhibits a rational, Renaissance inspiration. We shall take, as an example of a typical 16th-century square, Piazza Farnese, which is carefully thought out in proportion to the palazzo that dominates it. Piazza Navona, on the other hand, despite deriving its shape from the classical Stadium, is characteristically Baroque.

The Baroque square features a central decorative element on which it hinges and from which it takes its theme. Such an object might be an exceptional treasure of antiquity, like the obelisks or Marcus Aurelius' Column from which Piazza Colonna takes its name. The central element so completely embodies the theatrical spirit of the Baroque square that 19th-century squares like Piazza del Popolo and Piazza del Quirinale can logically be considered Baroque's highest expression.

Outstanding examples of the Rococo period, while different both in size and in aspect, are Piazza di Spagna and the smaller Piazza di Sant'Ignazio with its characteristic buildings that make it look exactly like a theater set.

Now comes the difficult task of suggesting a selection from the hundreds of churches and chapels built or rebuilt from the Renaissance onwards. We shall give one or two examples from each period but urge the reader to look out for the unexpected opportunity and to let curiosity guide the visitor's researches. We would merely like to propose some ecclesiastical buildings we consider essential to a sound knowledge of Rome.

Let us begin with the monumental churches. The link between Romanesque, Renaissance, and Baroque churches is provided by St. Mary over Minerva, the only example of Gothic architecture in Rome. Its decoration is, however, nearly all of later periods. In the main patriarchal basilicas, reconstruction has played a crucial role. St. Peter's was entirely remodeled, St. John in Lateran's interior was renovated by Borromini, and at Great St. Mary's, two regrettable chapels, the Sistine and the Borghese, have been added, as has an equally regrettable facade. The major Jesuit churches, Jesus' and St. Ignatius', must also be visited as they were the model for the Order's churches all over the world. We should also add St. Andrew-of-the-Valley, which echoes, on more modest lines, some of the features of St. Peter's; the New Church, with the adjoining Philippine Oratory; the scenic St. Gregory-on-the-Caelian; the 15th-century St. Mary-of-the-People; and St. Augustine's. There are also two of Borromini's jewels of graceful eccentricity, so different from St. Agnes in Agone, where Borromini was under the influence of other artists. These jewels are St. Carlino at the Four Fountains and St. Ivo's at the Sapienza. Next, we have the church of St. Andrew on the Quirinal, which Bernini's devotion brought forth, with its characteristic elliptical plan. Then, there are the twin churches near Trajan's Forum; St. Mary of Loreto, a miracle of the early Renaissance and topped by a whimsical lantern on its cupola; the 18th-century church of the Sacred Name of Mary; St. Mark's; St. Marcellus' on the Corso; and St. Mary's in Via Lata.

Finally, at the beginning of Via Venti Settembre, there are three ecclesiastical buildings, each of interest for a different reason. St. Bernard's is built in a rotunda from the Thermal Baths, St. Susanna's has sumptuous decorations on its walls, and St. Mary of the Victory is a rich bowl of delights with Bernini's ecstasy of St. Teresa. Nor can we forget, in the Borghi over towards the Vatican, the Church of the Transpontine and the Holy Spirit in Saxia, or St. Frances the Roman in the Roman Forum. All these suggestions could equally well be substituted by others. One notable element of these churches is the gilt, inlaid caisson ceilings, which became an essential feature of 16th-century decoration in all the major churches except those with a painted vault. These were often sumptuous with "glorias" that remind one of those in the drawing rooms and galleries of the most important families.

We should also mention the splendid sacristies, the altars, splendidly decorated with fine marble columns, and the many other furnishings, masterpieces of various crafts. We shall turn now to some of the smaller churches that boast outstanding decoration. The first of these "miniatures" is Bramante's chapel at St. Peter in Montorio, then Borromini's at St. John in Oil near the Porta Latina Gate, and St. Andrew's by Vignola on the Via Flaminia. Then there are the devotional churches of the guilds and confraternities, like St. Eligio of the Goldsmiths by Raffaello, St. Eligio of the Blacksmiths below the Capitol, and the Church of Prayer and Death in Via Giulia. The marvelous church of Mary Magdalene, not far from the Pantheon, whose splendid sacristy has a frivolous decoration more suited to a boudoir than to a church, is followed by St. Mary of Peace with its stupendous cloister dating from the 15th century, later graced with a lovely Baroque setting by Pietro da Cortona. The palazzos of Rome deserve equal attention, being a reinvention of the Florentine stylistic model from the period after the Middle Ages. Before that time, there had been only more-or-less temporary dwellings created among the ancient remains, the still modest residences of the cardinals adjoining the major churches and simple convents. Humanism elevated the "palazzo" to represent the external manifestation of a nobleman's dignity. In Rome, this normally meant Popes and cardinals. A few 15th-century examples look rather like fortresses, such as Palazzo Venezia and Palazzo dei Penitenzieri in Borgo Vecchio (today Via della Conciliazione), but then a richer, more serene style of building took over, of which the most outstanding example is the Palace of the Apostolic Chancellery, near Campo de' Fiori. However, apart from the Palace of the Roman College created for the Jesuit schools, and the three Capitol buildings, which together make up the most opulent Town Hall in the world, the great palazzos of the period are all of a dynastic nature. About 15 buildings are actually royal, in the sense that they belong to Papal dynasties. Of these "royal" palaces, we might mention Palazzo Farnese, Palazzo Pamphili in Piazza Navona, Palazzo Borghese, Palazzo Barberini, Palazzo Altieri, Palazzo Aldobrandini (now Palazzo Doria), Palazzo Rospigliosi, and Palazzo Corsini. These are the most important examples of architectural nepotism, but we cannot fail to mention that Palazzo Montecitorio and Palazzo Chigi (the lower house of the Italian parliament and the Italian prime minister's residence) have similar origins. The habit led to the formation in Rome of an architectural heritage of an extraordinarily high level, rivaled by the palazzos of the families of cardinals, like Palazzo Spada-Capodiferro, Palazzo Massimo alle Colonne, Palazzo Sciarra on the Corso, Palazzo Caetani-Ruspoli, and so on. The residences of the two major medieval families, the Colonnas and the Orsinis, are in a category apart. The Monte Giordano complex forms a Baroque camouflage for the original conglomerate of medieval fortifications, while the 15th-century building Peruzzi created over the Theater of Marcellus is a significant surviving example of a medieval structure built on top of more massive classical remains.

The great Baroque palazzos usually boast courtyards brightened by nymphs and interesting flights of stairs. The courtyard of Palazzo Farnese is solemn, that of the Palace of the Chancellery is calm, and that of Palazzo Borghese is particularly majestic. The roof terraces of the most important palazzos are worthy of mention as the last trace of the towers that once stood where they are now. They constitute an architectural feature whose purpose was both to provide panoramic views and to express noble pride. The three Papal palaces — the Vatican, the Lateran and the Quirinal — are outstanding for their sovereign grandeur, if not for their architectural merit. However, in deference to the theological precept that art with a religious content can be the most sublime expression of both genius and faith, they always reserved space for collections of art and antiquities, today gathered together in the Vatican Museums.

Emulating the Papal collections, all the great families had important collections of art, and their palazzos had "galleries" in which to display them. Some of these, like the Colonna, Doria-Pamphili and Spada galleries, are still *in situ.*

After the palazzos, it is logical to consider the major villa buildings. First, let us take the Chigi villa of the Farnesina, a successful example of the main pleasure lodges of Roman villas, all of which date from the Baroque period. Let us also mention the Aventine villa of the Order of Malta with its impressive history, its position, and Piranesi's architecture.

The Baroque and Renaissance periods dominate the overall picture of the city with their innumerable buildings, creating that synthesis of all the ages that we now know as Rome. Minor, but nonetheless important, aspects are the so-called "Madonnellas", of which there were 2000 at the end of the 18th century; the small place name-plaques; plaques announcing the name of a building's owner; those placed by the monsignor in charge of highways; and those commemorating the Tiber's high watermarks. All these are little flashes of Rome's history, important outward expressions of a vitality the Roman citizenry has always preserved, specific distinguishing features of humanity and good-natured folk wisdom. We should remember that the populace was not composed entirely of nobles and Papal officials. It remained separate, more of a spectator than a participant in the sumptuous theatrical

production staged in the Rome of the day. We cannot help but remember that the bitterly satirical society of the "mordant ironists" (speaking statues) grew up in the context of a majestic, unreal city. Pasquino, Morforio, Lucrezia, and its other exponents reserved a place, albeit in the chorus, for the people of Rome in that unique theatrical genre.

Rome - city of the world

There have always been cities that, because of certain traditional values, or a reputation for hard work or creativity in the fields of culture, art, or commerce, become points of reference for people beyond their geographical or political confines. In the ancient world, Rome stood out over other cities with great philosophical and artistic traditions, thanks to her ability to assimilate the best of the most diverse cultural and artistic movements. This situation was actually reversed with the arrival of Christianity as Rome became a center of the propagation of the new faith and the new ground rules of politics, a sort of ideal center of the medieval *res publica.* The Renaissance enhanced Rome's prestige as a place of culture and intellectual, particularly artistic, stimulation, to the point that the whole of Europe felt in some way "Roman". Men of faith and men of letters, scholars of Roman law, artists, and aesthetes all found inspiration, or rather, a congenial intellectual climate, at Rome. In the modern world, despite changes in the strictness of religious observance and in ecclesiastical discipline, in cultural fashions and artistic trends, Rome has not lost her fascination. Rome, the *patria communis* (common homeland), it was called; and this concept, underlined for some by the pilgrimage to the sources of faith and for others by the physical experience of historical or juridical tradition, took concrete shape in the foundation of many cultural and professional institutions. The most ancient moves in this direction were the *scholae,* national or professional guilds, which kept a permanent presence in Rome for the benefit of different groups of people. The *schola graeca* has left ample evidence of the vigorous Byzantine settlement from the seventh to the ninth century, in a series of churches with Oriental names between the *ripa graeca* (Greek Bank) of the Tiber and the Palatine, seat of the Dukes of Byzantium. The national-religious institutions of the northern peoples were to be found in the Borghi near St. Peter's, where they still remain, albeit more in the form of folk memories and place names than in any physical evidence. There were the settlements of the Franks, the Teutons, the Frisians, and the Saxons. The Teutonic settlement is, indeed, still extant behind the sacristy of St. Peter's with its ancient cemetery. At the edge of the slopes of the Janiculum, we find the church of Saints Michael and Magnus of the Frisians with its holy steps, and the great hospital block of the Holy Spirit "in Saxia". The charm of these places is literally beyond description. They sprang up near the sites where the early evangelists of the faith that transformed European civilization's cultural and psychological foundations suffered martyrdom and were buried. As one discovers the history behind the various sites, one comprehends the moment of spiritual fusion that created the Europe of the soul underpinning contemporary society. Examples may be found at St. Gregory-on-the-Caelian, where the evangelizing Pope, St. Gregory the Great, lived and worked; or in the monastery district on the Aventine; or in the area of the ancient Patriarchate, whose only surviving element today is the Sancta Sanctorum.

Whenever contemporary Europe feels drawn towards unity, it may not always be obvious that the impulse derives from roots that peoples, today distinct, once shared. One of the places that excite this strong urge is underground at the church of St. Clement's where, among many other points of interest, lies the tomb of Cyril, the bishop who launched the appeal for unity with Eastern Europe.

After the early national settlements, under the protection of Emperors and sovereigns and the benevolence of Popes, there came another series of institutions destined to provide assistance to various national communities, to furnish both care and cure, to foster study and prayer. These were no longer on the edge of the city but deep in its Renaissance heart. Their aims were carried out thanks to holdings whose income they received and together, both institutions and holdings took the name of the "Establishments" of their respective countries. The English Establishments were looted after the creation of the Church of England, but the Teutonic Establishments continued to thrive and were joined by the Establishments of peoples of imperial countries, the French and the Spanish, both considered prestigious political and cultural presences as well as a means of putting subtle diplomatic pressure on the Papacy. The national Establishments were based around monumental buildings, not necessarily religious, as well as impressive headquarters distinguished not, as in ancient times, by franchises and immunity, but by a sort of moral oneness with their respective homelands.

Other institutions might be added to the list of national Establishments, like St. Jerome of the Illyrians with its adjoining hospice, St. Julian Hospitaller of the Belgians, the Hospice of the Bohemians, St. Anastasius of the Greeks, St. Isidore of the Irish, St. Stanislaus of the Poles, St. Anthony of the Portuguese, St. Brigid of the Swedes, St. Stephen the Round of the Hungarians, St. Nicholas of the Lorrainers, and St. Claude of the Burgundians. They are all places of worship or monuments in the center of Rome with important artistic contributions, often distinguished by the typical artistic styles of their patrons' homeland.

Similar to the foreign institutions were those of the various regions of Italy, represented at Rome by marvelous places of worship. We might note St. Mark of the Venetians, St. John of the Florentines, St. John of the Genoese, St. Catherine of the Sienese, St. Bonaventura of the Luccans, the Church of the Shroud of the Piedmontese and Nicois, St. Mary of Itria of the Sicilians, the church of St. Ambrose and St. Charles of the Lombards, St. Saviour in Lauro of the Marches, St. Petronius of the Bolognese, St. Francis of Paola of the Calabrians, the Church of the Holy Spirit of the Neapolitans, St. Bartholomew of the Bergamasks, and St. Mary of Monterone of the Umbrians. These churches usually feature adjoining hospices of outstanding importance, housed in monumental or historic buildings.

The older buildings are usually of a religious nature but they were joined, from the Renaissance onwards, by cultural institutions whose archetype is to be found in the Academy of France, founded at Rome by Colbert. Originally intended for artists, these institutions have more recently begun to widen their scope, providing a base for the studies not only of young people but also of more mature scholars. Other cultural institutions, entirely dedicated to archaeological or archive research, were set up after the Vatican Archives were opened to scholars by Leo XIII. More have been added to the list in recent decades, especially after the decision to encourage their establishment in the special area set aside for them in the so-called Julian Valley. A host of countries, many themselves of recent constitution, have set up cultural institutions, but only the oldest can boast architecturally important buildings.

The Guilds of Arts and Crafts were also most welcoming to those who plied their trade in Rome. They generally had headquarters based at a church, such as Saints Luke and Marina in the Roman Forum, the Academy of St. Luke and the church of St. Laurence in Miranda, in the Temple of Antoninus and Faustina, or that of the College of Spicemakers. There are also many lesser churches linked to trades, from St. Barbara of the Booksellers to St. Omobono of the Tailors, St. Eligio of the Goldsmiths and St. Eligio of the Blacksmiths to St. Mary of the Garden for victuallers and related trades.

Devotional confraternities were open to strangers residing in Rome, too, and they have left their mark all over the city. The plaques proclaiming the ownership of buildings, for instance, are famous, such as those of the Confraternity of the Banner, whose Oratory near Via Giulia is now a lovely musical auditorium, or those of the Confraternity of the Sancta Sanctorum.

The Academies were open to foreigners, having been created at the express wish of one herself a foreigner, Queen Christine of Sweden. Many foreign scholars belonged to the Lincei Academy which, today, is the leading national academy. At the Sapienza, the Roman university founded by Boniface VIII, there was a constant presence of foreign teachers and students as, indeed, there was at the Roman College, the complex of Jesuit schools that grew up at the end of the 16th century. The Sapienza and the Roman College are, moreover, of outstanding architectural merit.

The cultural, artistic, and craft world at Rome had an international dimension that received stimulation and support from the Papal See, itself international in outlook, and from the sovereigns who prided themselves on protecting their subjects and on making donations; for example, the Arcadian Academy was a gift of John V of Portugal. A further international aspect was, of course, the creative contribution of the artists and craftsmen who worked in Rome for long or short periods of time, taking part in the completion of the city's monuments and even starting artistic movements. We might note landscape painting, the greatest exponents of which were the French artists, Lorrain, Poussin, and Corot; the school of Flemish panoramic artists; the Flemish and Neapolitan followers of Peter van Laer, called il Bamboccio (the Chubby Child); the northern "Nazarene" movement; and so on. For this reason, Rome is to be considered a joint creation of many artists, few of whom were Roman.

Some areas of Rome are indissolubly linked to the memory of a period spent there by some great person, such as Villa delle Rose, which belonged to Ludwig of Bavaria; the red house in Piazza di Spagna with its memorial to Keats and Byron; the museum-house of Goethe on the Corso; and the studios in the Via Sistina where a succession of 18th- and 19th-century artists, Italian and foreign, lived. The list would be very long indeed, as the commemorative plaques all over the city remind us. All of the foregoing would seem to have led to a sort of psychological dependence on Rome of a huge swathe of culture, from the highest levels down to the most popular. The situation is changing, as humanistic and historic values decay both at school, and in society at large with its new technical and scientific myths, not to mention philosophical and literary values that are empirical where they are not actually materialistic. Despite all this, and quite apart from run-of-the-mill mass tourism, pilgrimages of faith and culture are still made by large numbers of people and are still the dominant feature in the overall profile of visitors to Rome.

Religious pilgrimages were the main motive behind large-scale contacts with Rome in the past. These produced evident signs of influence on the city's appearance with the institutions that sprang up to accommodate the pilgrims and the sites they came to visit. Over the centuries, the Jubilee was the most typical and most powerful of the reasons for pilgrimages, but it was also a stimulus to new building and revised town planning. Every 25 years the Jubilee caused waves of restoration and restructuring as well as special initiatives. A few examples are the construction of the Sistine Bridge in 1475, the foundation of the Hospice for Pilgrims and Convalescents for the Jubilee of 1675, and the building of the original part of Via del Babuino in 1525. In fact, every district and monument in Rome bears some mark of the succession of Jubilee years. The rediscovery of the catacombs and the creation of the catacomb basilicas were certainly due to Jubilee activity, especially along the itinerary of the Seven Churches. This route found an enthusiastic sponsor and a fertile source of ideas for ceremony in Filippo Neri. Furthermore, the many tombs of foreigners in the churches are explained by the Jubilee and other pilgrimages, as is that singular survivor of ancient times, the little cemetery of St. Andrew, on the right bank of the Tiber near the Milvian Bridge. An association of ideas leads us, at this point, to mention a spot wrapped in an aura of eternal Romanticism, the so-called English Cemetery, established for non-Catholic foreigners in a secluded area near the city walls. Such pilgrims came to visit Rome, rather than the Christian sanctuaries, and then died by chance here, although many had chosen to live in Rome and wished to be buried one day in Roman soil.

Rome the capital

The outward signs of the 120 years for which Rome has been the capital of Italy are clearly visible on the city's features. Buildings designed to impress occupy some of the high ground while building development has proceeded apace in all directions, towards the hills and towards the sea, bringing the area called the "Roman countryside" into the conurbation. New roads crisscross the ancient fabric of the city while avenues and main roads reach out to city horizons once undreamt of. The city has suffered two kinds of profound transformations, the intentional ones stemming from the proclamation of Rome as capital, which take little account of Rome's traditional nature, and the transformations resulting in part from the new status and in part from the increase in population and the advent of industry.

Some of the latter would have occurred inevitably, whatever measures had been taken to safeguard the ancient city. The restructuring undertaken at the time of Pius IX, including the selection of a site for the railway terminus, the creation of the present Via Nazionale, some timid building in the Prati area, and the building of Piazza Mastai in Trastevere state clearly an intention to effect other changes. We should not decry the fact that these were often inspired by cultural insensibility and ideological prejudice. The Italian Rome, wrongly, did not create a parallel, autonomous modern city, but could at least have based its choices on respect for the past. We have come to this conclusion now, after a century of mistakes, and can suggest new perspectives on the past by juxtaposing, cautiously, vital forms of modern expression and ancient remains. Indiscriminate demolition, and the preferential treatment given to classical remains — which would have been rediscovered in any case — while destroying everything on top of them, were regrettable. The concept was a hangover from the theories and initiatives of the Napoleonic period in Rome, later to be dusted off in Paris by Baron Haussman in a context of centralized town planning and ample financial resources.

The anachronistic methods adopted in setting up the capital at Rome probably destroyed more landmarks and townscapes than they created. Let the memory of the port of Ripetta and the total destruction of other urban environments of great character like Via dei Pontefici, the Augusteum, and the area of the slopes of the Capitol symbolize all the other jewels now lost for ever.

Rome's appearance changed most, in the period when she became capital, as a result of the necessary construction of the gray defensive embankments raised against the Tiber's floods. These are two rough, long ramparts that no one thought to enliven with structural variations or decoration. Other significant public works in this respect were the opening of Corso Vittorio Emanuele, which broke up a compact urban zone; the development of the villa parklands, especially at Villa Ludovisi; and some of the large scale demolition, such as that for the Vittoriano; and the later demolition of the Fascist period to create Via della Conciliazione. The reclamation of the Ghetto was of extreme importance and was rounded off by the building of the new Synagogue with its Oriental-style dome.

Some of the old Rome's most sadly typical views, left behind by the Middle Ages, disappeared. These environmental abominations can be seen in pictures from the turn of the century, but it would have been better to use a chisel, rather than a pick, to extract and preserve the jewels that lay hidden in the slums. It would, however, be mere decadent romanticism to cry over the idealized past when it was characterized by such misery and inner-city decay. Moreover, the present generation has allowed *its* heritage of natural and historical beauty in the surrounding countryside to be carelessly tossed away and therefore has little right to point out the errors of the past.

Many conversions of open spaces and buildings have thrown up new perspectives that sometimes exalt ancient monuments, giving a wider scope to certain traditional views. This is the case in the Renaissance quarters, where "thinning out" has had notably positive visual results.

The period of King Humbert has left particularly noticeable marks on the city center. The white colossus of the Vittoriano was deliberately designed to impose upon the townscape an alternative to so many other monuments heavy with a history that was thought irrelevant. The dome of the Vatican was to have been mortified by this sort of eighth — marble — hill of Rome, while the Capitol was actually wiped off the view from the most prestigious point of entry into Rome, Piazza del Popolo.

The chalky Palace of Justice is also graceless, but the overloaded decoration of its facades does convey the taste of a definite period of history. Corso Vittorio has a distinctly Humbertine flavor as a result of the restructuring of many of its buildings. The area between the beautifully designed Piazza dell'Esedra and Largo di Magnanapoli, on the other hand, is more coherently of that period. The area of the Praetorian Guard Barracks, Piazza Vittorio, and the Prati district are of the same period. Much building went on in an eclectic style of political inspiration, which held that the new Italy was to spring from the blending of different regional schools.

Koch's work provides the most important examples of this – his Esedra palazzo, Bank of Italy, Palazzo Margherita. The Palazzo Odescalchi on the Corso, Palazzo Simonetti in Via Vittoria Colonna, Palazzo Brancaccio, and the side facade of the Piccola Farnesina palazzo in Corso Vittorio are all worthy of note. Even if the town planning and buildings of the Humbertine period are the object of after-dinner "demolition orders" from those who judge such matters ideologically and with the benefit of hindsight, we believe they furnish the collector of visual impressions of Rome with an important side of the modern city, by no means always unworthy of its panoramic past. One need only mention the sinuous elegance of Via Veneto or the graceful sweep of Corso d'Italia along the walls, and the great shady avenues from those in Prati to those in Parioli, or main roads like Via Nazionale or Via Cola di Rienzo to see a 19th-century city worthy of being a capital. It is in any case more useful to linger over the town planning, rather than the architectural, aspect of the Humbertine period although it did produce distinguished private buildings with palazzos and family residences of a dignity that was later to be lost. Subsequently, the "palazzina" type of residence that would characterize the post-Second World War period was introduced. This interrupted the tradition of great, compact blocks and the linear continuity of many buildings standing together shoulder to shoulder, which was both pleasing to the eye and expressed a philosophy of social solidarity.

Here, we could mention the late 19th-century veneer that modest conversions or the abundant availability of visual documentation from the period has foisted on spaces which belong to other periods. This is the case with Piazza Colonna, the drawing room of turn-of-the-century Rome, and Piazza del Popolo with its carnival parties and catherine wheels alight on the Pincio terrace.

The modest level of building, as if the creativity of past ages had dried up, dragged on into subsequent periods in the form of the many ministerial buildings, and in the shape of what was to have been a monument to the contemporary expressive spirit, the Colonna Gallery. It lacks any real grandeur.

The Fascist period, while lavishing attention on Rome from the scenic point of view, did not produce buildings of any note. The Art Nouveau revisitations have no originality and neither do the Baroque ones, while the attempts at creating a 20th-century style by and large fail. Only some of the EUR buildings merit a mention (the Palace of Civilization and the Palace of Congress), but even they are forced to cohabit, against nature and logic, with the prevailing imperialist views of architecture. Such views were characterized by inhumanly vast colonnades that reveal a conceptual vacuum and a sterile political attitude. Some interest might be derived from the impressive buildings of the university campus or the beauty of the Foro Italico, which respects the natural environmental setting. The deliberate monumentalism of the building that is now the Foreign Ministry is, however, mere repetitive multiple giantism. The collection of visual experiences is certainly destined to take up less space than the naked gladiators bearing symbols of various sports who stand out against the soft hill of Monte Mario over the marble stadium.

Over the last 40 years, Rome's territory has vastly increased and there have been many opportunities to produce new beauty in complete independence of style. Sadly, no praiseworthy works of architecture have been erected, nor have pleasant environments been created using trees or appropriate furniture. Apart from a few areas of the EUR, we cannot nominate very much. It is as if everything has happened by chance in the absence of adequate coordination, although this should have been possible even if funds were limited. Unfortunately, panoramic areas of note, like those on the Parioli and Monte Mario hills, have been degraded by a development lacking in imagination, which has suffocated them. We would like to be able to say that at least religious architecture has distinguished itself in the wake of the liturgical innovations, given that there has been no lack of opportunity for taking the broader view. Many such opportunities have, however, been wasted in rehashing the most pedestrian traditionalism in clumsy linear arrangements. On this flat panorama, the church of Saints Peter and Paul at the EUR stands out for sheer monumentality, as does the church of the Canadian Martyrs at Piazza Bologna, where reinforced concrete has served creativity well. The church of Don Bosco in the Tuscolano district and, in the eastern development area, the parish church of Tor Bella Monaca are also worth seeing. It is not easy to shake off the burden of the historic greatness of the sacred architecture that dominates the city.

The stupendous area around Rome is home to important classical and medieval sites, always fascinating and always "Roman", to be highlighted in special corners of memory. The area also enjoys the enviable panoramic resources of this part of the Lazio region between the hills and the sea. It is quite possible to create a new balance between functionality and beauty with new views of the cityscape, the message of its eternal nature defining new monumental symbols to place alongside those of more fruitful times.

Armando Ravaglioli

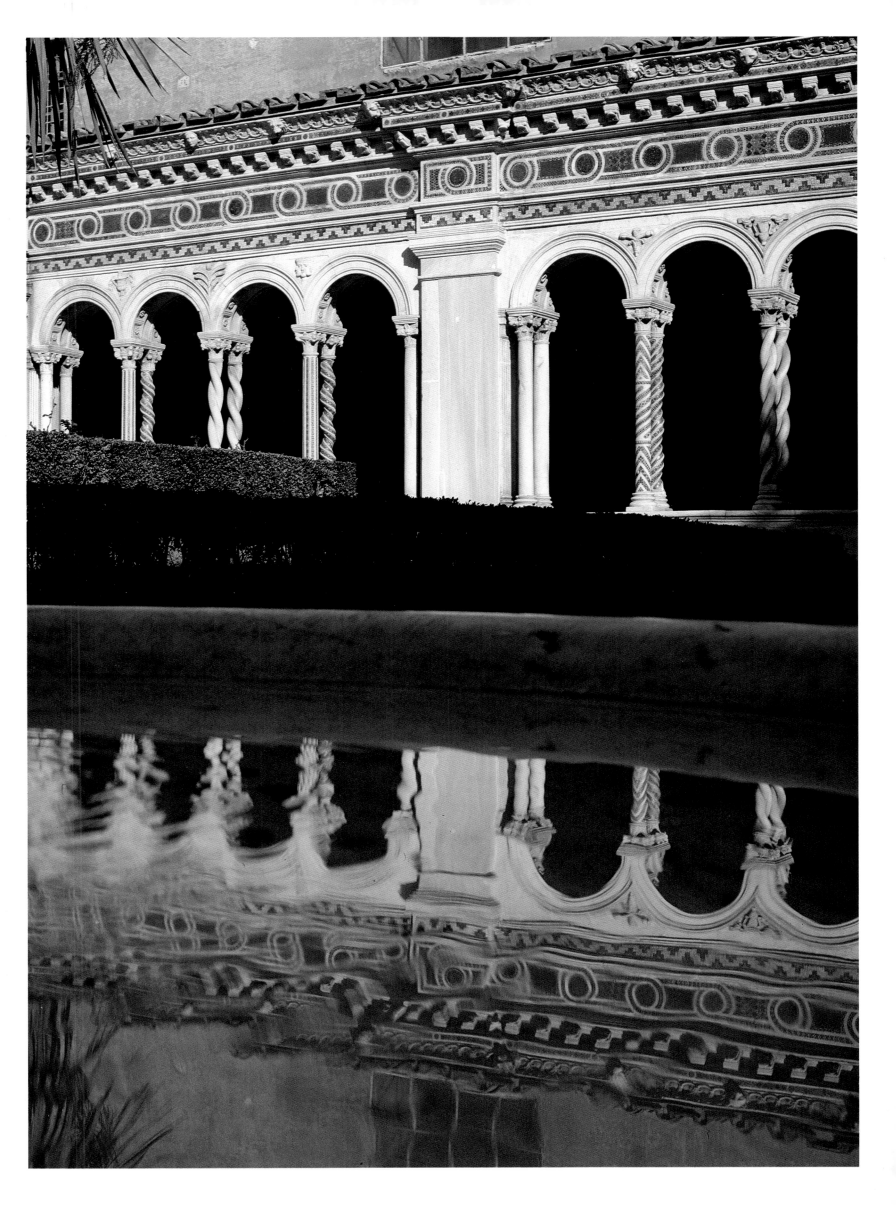

IONAS

A straight stretch of the **Via Appia Antica** beyond Capo di Bove (the famous tomb of Cecilia Metella). Rome is perhaps unique, with its many different incarnations, in being able to suggest a link with the hereafter. Romanticism and Classicism exalted this ancient road in the 19th century for conflicting, but convergent, reasons. Travelers arriving from Magna Graecia reviewed the funerary monuments of the great families as they passed by.

The **Vale of the Forum** from the slopes of the Capitol. The Forum Romanum remained the real public square in Rome even after the building of the splendid Imperial Forums, which can just be made out on the left. Here, in the formerly marshy hollow reclaimed among the legendary hills, jostled temples and civic basilicas. We can still trace their lines in the rebuilt versions erected at the height of Rome's glory.

A detail of the **Triumphal Arch of Septimius Severus** against the background of the church of Saints Luke and Martina. The present-day square is on a higher level than the ancient Forum Romanum, indicating how modern Rome is built on top of the rubble of ancient buildings. The two monuments, although separated in time by many centuries, are brought together by the emphatic, celebratory nature of Baroque architecture.

The focal point of the **Forum Romanum** was the Comitium, a small open space between the Julian (the modest remains on the left) and the Emilian (on the right, under the church of Saints Luke and Martina) Basilicas. This unassuming area was surrounded by imposing buildings, mainly votive constructions dedicated to various gods. The three columns in the foreground belong to the Temple of the Dioscuri, bearers of victory at the battle of Lake Regillus.

Water lilies in flower in the still waters of the entrance to the **House of the Vestals,** the chaste priestesses of the Sacred Fire in the nearby Temple of Vesta. The Vestals were the very cream of ancient Roman womanhood and received an education that entitled them to much honor and respect for their political judgement. In this way, they mirrored the position of the Nymph, Egeria, who inspired Numa Pompilius.

Paganism followed by Christianity. The elegant **dome of the Church of the Sacred Name of Mary** rises above the reassembled **columns of the Temple of Venus** (Caesar's Forum is on the right). The church was built to offer thanks for Sobieski's victory over the Turks at Vienna (1683). On the left, **Trajan's Column** no longer bears the Emperor's statue, but instead a 16th-century statue of St. Peter.

Detail of **Trajan's Column.** The warrior ancestors of today's Romans in the lands of the Danube. This golden-age carving employed countless artesans to recount the deeds of the great Emperor. In addition to its original commemorative function, it provides a documentary account of life in the military camps, on the march, and in battle, and of the cruelty and the clemency of the Roman army.

Detail of the **Ara Pacis,** reassembled in 1938 in front of the Mausoleum of Augustus. The altar dedicated to the world peace re-established by the first Emperor stands in a marble enclosure. Six figurative panels top a base and a molding of floral spirals. The two longest panels, on the sides, depict a procession of the imperial family with Augustus at its head.

Rising over this expanse of glory is the **Chariot of Victory.** The Vittoriano stands like a backdrop for an outstanding monumental composition. On the left, the apse of Ara Coeli; below, St. Joseph of the Carpenters (the church of the Guild of Carpenters, above the Mamertine Prison); then the dome erected by Pietro da Cortona for the church of the Guild of Artists (Saints Luke and Martina). These are followed by the Curia building and St. Laurence in Miranda, in the colonnade of the Temple of Antoninus and Faustina.

The **Arch of Constantine,** the last great commemorative public work of ancient Rome. It was built after the victory at the Milvian Bridge but its great, noble lines reveal that the glory of Rome was fast ebbing away. Columns, statues and medallions salvaged from other monuments were used in its construction. The outline of the splendid fountain called the *Meta Sudans* (sweating winning-post) can be traced in front. The fountain was removed under the Fascist government in 1936.

The **Arch of Titus** lies at the top of the Via Sacra, which came down to the Vale of the Forum from the slopes of the Palatine Hill. The Arch was erected by Domitian in memory of his brother, Titus, and commemorates the destruction of the Temple of Jerusalem and the diaspora of the Jewish people. Underneath, the remains of famous monuments are picked out against the Palazzo Senatorio as if they were laid out on a giant chessboard. In the background can be seen the arches of the *Tabularium,* the ancient Archives of State.

The walls may have been stripped of their precious marble, but the rooms look as if people were milling around here just a few moments ago. This austere area of the **Thermal Baths of Caracalla,** beautified by the mosaic floor, is one of the many ancient Roman remains that give the impression that this ancient way of life could start up again at once after an interval of many centuries.

The ancient **Via Biberatica** in the area known as Trajan's Markets. The road meanders between restored ancient buildings, as if wandering round a bazaar waiting for the sellers to call from their workshops. The road divides the unique building that goes from Trajan's Forum to the Quirinal Hill into two separate parts, each of three stories.

The **Colosseum** in a whirl of light. The lights of the vehicles look like fire bursting out in the night with the intensity of midsummer sunshine. The amphitheater appears larger than ever as the arches rush up from level to level. To think that the Hospital of St. John, one of the first in the world, kept going by selling off part of the travertine stone brought down by earthquakes! This is grandeur of a different order than that of our skyscrapers.

Oleanders in blossom against the **arcades of the Colosseum.** This plant's lack of thirst suits it admirably for the hot Roman summer. The photograph is taken against the internal circle of the amphitheater, at the Caelian hill side, where disasters and human greed have removed the external wall of the structure. There were 80 arches in the wall to ensure a rapid, easy flow of spectators in and out.

An aerial view of the central archaeological zone from the **Capitol to the Forum Romanum, the Imperial Forums, the Palatine, the Caelian** and **the Oppio Hill.** This immense openair museum hinges on the huge oval of the Colosseum, built in the valley where the lake of the Domus Aurea had lain. The present-day Via dei Fori Imperiali cannot, of course, continue to be a main thoroughfare but neither can it be transformed into an archaeological site that would stifle the life of the city.

The bowels of the **Colosseum.** Archaeologists, astounded by the sophisticated use of the space beneath the amphitheater's stalls, make us look at the Colosseum in a way Quintus Aterius, its likely builder, never imagined it could be seen. Machinery took wild beasts and scenery up to the floor of the arena that, like the terraces, was protected by an immense curtain wall.

These remains in the **Hippodrome of the Palatine Imperial Palace** are a puzzle for archaeologists. They are thought to belong to a construction, from the time of Theodoric, that changed the whole nature of the arena. This group of remains which has come to light on the hill is a source of great interest to scholars but many people regret the lost charm of the romantic scenes that were once to be enjoyed here.

The **Canope of Hadrian's Villa.** The Villa is an extraordinary "world in miniature" with its scale reproductions of the most famous buildings of the ancient East, as the Emperor Hadrian had admired them. We find a complex of residential palaces, thermal baths, porticoes, nymphaeums, lakes and theaters. Villa d'Este, which looks down from the heights of Tivoli, is the result of a desire to imitate that, while unable to compete in grandeur, more than holds its own in the use of water displays.

The **Roman Theater of ancient Ostia,** opposite Piazzale delle Corporazioni. Partially adapted to enable the staging of highly evocative shows, it echoes the incomparable fascination of the archaeological site surrounding it. The city of Ostia is a kind of Pompei, not destroyed but merely abandoned, and still capable of showing us how a long-dead life-style was lived. A visit to Ostia, once the port of Rome, completes a visit to the Rome of ancient times.

Part of the northern semicircle of the **Forum of Augustus.** This edifice is a good example of the reuse of the major ancient monuments in Rome's continuing development. Over the remaining traces of ancient decoration rise a triple window of Gothic inspiration and cruciform windows from the late 15th century. These commemorate the establishment of the Knights of Rhodes, later the Knights of Malta, on the ancient site.

Agrippa's Pantheon, here clothed in summer flowers, is one of the great symbols of the way that ancient Rome lives alongside the modern city. The edifice was first an anthology of pagan cults, then housed the bones of the early Christian martyrs recovered from the catacombs, and finally, after the burial here of Raffaello, became a resting place for the greatest artists and also for royalty.

The interior of **St. Constance's Mausoleum,** an artistically outstanding monument with a controversial history. It was not designed as a place of worship, but as a great mausoleum for the Emperor Constantine's daughter. For a long time it was thought to be a Temple of Bacchus because of its mosaic decorations with their theme of life and wine, in fact taken from Christian symbolism. The perfect sense of space and the superb mosaics in the vaults make it much sought after today for wedding ceremonies.

Detail of the **cloister of St. Paul-outside-the-walls,** together with the Lateran cloister, the finest in the city. Both are the work of the Vassalletto family of Roman marble masons. The renaissance in the early centuries of the new millennium produced at Rome a fine chool of artists and one of mosaic art, whose highest expression was in the marble masons' work. These craftsmen laid carpets of multicolored stones in the church naves, also decorating the columns and tombs.

The central nave of **St. John Lateran,** Rome's and the world's cathedral. The ancient basilica escaped the fate of St. Peter's in the Vatican because Borromini, instead of demolishing it, incorporated its columns and arches into the naves in imposing pillars with niches, reliefs, and paintings in the exuberant Baroque style. In the lesser naves, elements of the ancient wall and decorative furnishings are preserved.

Piazza Santa Maria in Trastevere. The Romanesque bell tower with its shrine and mosaic dedicated to Mary is framed between the ancient basin of the 15th-century fountain and the 19th-century crest. Beneath the gable of the church, a splendid mosaic fascia awaits the evening light. The color and charm of the district are everywhere intact. In the 15th century, Trastevere was still alien to Rome, yet now some visitors regard it as the most authentic quarter.

The basilica of **St. Mary in Cosmedin,** whose beautiful name isredolent of Byzantium, with its superb Romanesque bell tower decorated with multi-colored Saracen arches. Inside, the massive remains of the ancient Corn Supply Office that housed the original Christian deaconry await us. Bizzoccheri's 18th-century fountain, with its two Tritons and their intertwining tails, dominates the photograph. The fountain is one of Rome's most charming pieces of urban decoration.

The so-called **Paradise Chapel**, dedicated to St. Zeno, at the **Church of St. Praxedes'**. Dating from the early ninth century, the chapel is an outstanding example of Byzantine culture and bears witness to the long Eastern domination of Rome. In the middle of a solid gold vault, a circle depicting Christ in the act of benediction is supported by four solemn angels that extend the line of the four corner pillars.

The Gallery of Palazzo Farnese is the triumphal conclusion of work on the monumental palace for Cardinal Alessandro Farnese, later pope with the name of Paul III. The internal decoration, besides the frescoes by Francesco Salviati and Taddeo Zuccari, attains its highest level of expression in the gallery which Carracci brothers frescoed stupendously with mythological subjects such as *The Triumph of Bacchus and Arianne*.

Moro's fountain in Piazza Navona, by G. A. Mari upon Bernini's design. Placed along the edges of the tub are tritons, dolphins and fanciful masks. Cafes, restaurants, art galleries, amateur artists and musicians, along with the pleasant splashing sound of the water make Piazza Navona an ideal place for relaxation, far away from the everyday commotion and tasks of a large metropolis.

The *schola cantorum* of **St. Clement's** and the calotte of the apse with the mosaic of the triumph of the Cross (first half of the 12th century). The church documents one of Rome's greatest catastrophes, the devastating conflagration started by Robert Guiscard (1084). Pope Pascal II decided to abandon and cover over the previous basilica in 1108. Today, it may be visited thanks to the 19th-century excavations that brought an entire ancient district to light.

A happy choice of **viewpoint from the terrace of Castel Sant'Angelo** has allowed our photographer to compose this unusual variation on the "skyline" theme. Against the backdrop of the Alban Hills, the bulk of the Vittoriano is offset by the domes of St. Savior in Lauro and St. Agnes', while a change of rhythm at the Ara Coeli picks out the spiral of St. Ivo at the Sapienza and the spire of the Anima.

In this detail of the **Fountain of Rivers in Piazza Navona** the symbolic personification of the river *Ganges* stands out against the vigorous lines of the **Church of St. Agnes in Agone**. This church, conceived as the court chapel for the princely Pamphilj Palace, recalls a bloody martyrdom in the ancient Stadium of Domitian, upon which the present square took form. Borromini's concave facade, however, alters the original lines of the Stadium's terracing.

Michelangelo's *Moses* **at St. Peter-in-Chains,** one of the most imposing pieces of sculpture ever executed. It was to have been part of the huge tomb Pope Julius II had planned for himself but is more than enough to perpetuate the glory of artist and patron on its own. The legendary mark left on its knee by the hammer blow that was to have brought it to life cannot be made out.

Via Condotti is one of Rome's most impenetrable mysteries. This straight, narrow street between the Pincio hill and the Tiber manages to outdo competition from the world's most renowned shopping streets. Only the atmosphere of Rome with its grand settings and intimate spaces can explain the mystery. The most important stylists in the world of fashion meet here in Via Condotti.

The **Fountain of Trevi.** Virgin water was thought worthy of this display, the greatest celebration of water ever made. It is a symphony modulated by the cascades, a lyric composition in stone made poetry. It was the return to Rome of this ancient Water, begun in 1453, that marked the city's revival and the start of the Renaissance. Three centuries and vast amounts of money were needed to complete what is today a supremely effective tourist attraction.

The **Capitol** illuminated by "Roman torches". On Christmas Day and on major public holidays, this spectacular illumination of Capitol Square takes place. The reddish glow of the *padelloni* (great pans) highlights Michelangelo's architecture in what is more a theatrical stage than a public square. In the center, a small, but magnificent, protagonist holds sway – the equestrian statue of Marcus Aurelius.

The steps of **Trinità dei Monti** under the azaleas. For 40 years, this setting has been showered every spring with all the colors of the season's flowers. It is a suitable scene above all for the fashion parades that Roman stylists hold here every year. The steps have also, in recent years, become a ritual meeting place of the younger generation on their happy-go-lucky globe-trotting modern-day equivalent of the "Grand Tour".

The **Fountain of the Triton** reminds us of Gian Lorenzo Bernini and the Barberini family at the end of a 19th-century street that formed one of the main arteries of the new city, wiping out a tangle of back streets. The fabulous protagonist launches a thin jet of water from his bugle into the sky. The illuminated hoardings, however, make it look feeble by comparison. The fountain was to have stood in a kind of rustic courtyard under the palazzo.

Capitol Square bathed in light and seen from the staircase leading up to the main door of the Palazzo Senatorio. Beyond the edge of the stage marked out by two groups of Dioscuri, the indistinct panorama of the city unfolds. This is the *Urbs* (City), almost a synonym of *Orbis* (Globe). The creators of the square - Pope Paul III Farnese and Michelangelo Buonarroti - knew they were creating a setting in which the whole world could admire Rome's ancient and modern splendor.

The photographer's virtuosity gives us an unusual view of the group of **twin cupolas in Piazza del Popolo,** along with the **obelisk** placed there by Sextus V as the top of the Trident formed by Via del Babuino, Via del Corso, and Via Ripetta. The obelisk blocks the Corso in a highly spectacular fashion but prevents any repetition of the Barberi races.

Panoramic view of the **Palatine looking towards the Capitol,** with monuments from many different periods. In the background, the Byzantine church of St. Theodore and the walls of the *horrea* (granaries) of Agrippina. There follows the squat bulk of the Curia. Via dei Fienili at the bottom is an extension of the ancient Vicus Tuscus. In the background are the Capitol buildings, from Palazzo Caffarelli to Palazzo Senatorio and on to the strange white bulk of the Vittoriano and the Torre delle Milizie.

"Minerva's Chick". The small elephant, designed to support the Egyptian obelisk that was rather too small for the square, comes from a fantastic, totally unrealistic bestiary. The popular imagination chose to fall back on the hen-house, rather than the memory of a famous elephant that had visited Rome a century previously. In this, as in so many other things, pretension was brought down to earth by popular wit.

The **Fountain of the Tortoises** (or Young Boys). The most graceful fountain in Rome, and the most agreeable of the dozen designed by Giacomo Della Porta. This is the only one to make use of bronze sculptures. The author, Tommaso Landolfi, wove one of his fantasies around the graceful movements of the young boys and the tortoises drawn towards the basin.

The *Triumph of Divine Providence,* or the apotheosis of the Barberinis. This is the theme elaborated in the 500 square meters of fresco in the vault of the main hall of Palazzo Barberini. It is the masterpiece of Pietro da Cortona, one of the most important Baroque architects and artists. The fresco forms part of the collection of the National Gallery of Ancient Art, now housed in the palazzo.

The *Sarcophagus of the Bride and Groom* in the National Museum of Valle Giulia. This Etruscan collection, together with that in the Vatican Museum, makes Rome the most important center for Etruscan remains. "Tuscia" was, after all, at the root of Roman civilization from the time of the Tarquins, when its contribution helped to enable Rome to establish her cultural and political superiority over neighboring peoples.

Beyond the central arch of the **Sant'Angelo Bridge** the majestic dome of St. Peter's stands out. The three central arches of the bridge date back to the imperial period, while the two outer ones were added in the seventeenth century. Built for the Emperor Hadrian who wanted to connect his mausoleum to the left bank of the Tiber, together with the Ponte Rotto bridge it constitutes one of the most important relics of ancient Roman roadway architecture.

A modern-day novelty – **St. Peter's Square** as a reception room. Modern transport brings to Rome crowds of pilgrims all year round in numbers previously only seen in Holy Years. St. Peter's Square, which stands where the ancient atrium of the basilica stood, continuously plays host to the huge crowds that come to see the Pope celebrate Mass on the forecourt of the basilica, or appear at the loggia to bless worshippers, or, more intimately, wave from the window of his study.

The **Capitol She-wolf**, the heraldic animal of Rome that replaced the eagles and the lion. The wild, maternal she-wolf seems to express the nature of the ancient domination of the world by Rome, which was sure and decisive but also encouraged the formation of new civil orders and new nations. The tablets in the Hall of the Fasti around the bronze Etruscan statue are the august remains of the ancient lists of magistrates displayed in the Forum.

The statues of the angels bearing the symbols of the Passion along the **Sant'Angelo Bridge** as a group constitute an example of the most elegant Roman Barocco. Conceived by Gian Lorenzo Bernini and constructed by his pupils, the array of ten angels holding the symbols of the Passion of Christ anticipates the sight of Archangel Michael positioned at the top of Hadrian's mausoleum.

A classic view of the city from the dome of St. Peter's. A long line of holy figures, from the Redeemer to the Apostles and the most important witnesses of the Christian faith, surrounds the square in an embrace and welcomes the crowds arriving along the huge approach of Via della Conciliazione and Piazza Pio XII. This uplifting scene forces its way into the little world of the "Borghi" (which survives on the left) and the hospices and hospitals that have come to us directly from the Middle Ages (on the right).

The *Esquiline Venus* is one of the most precious pieces in the Capitoline collections. Depicting a naked young girl tying her hair up in a band, it emerged in the last century from the excavations at Orti Lamiani on the Esquiline Hill. Orti Lamiani was one of the villas of ancient Rome where the belt of gardens (*orti*) and pleasure lodges had grown up. These were removed without ceremony to make way for new developments when Rome became the capital city of Italy.

Castel Sant'Angelo, the great mausoleum served as a burial place for members of the Imperial family up until Caracalla. Despite the alterations carried out on the structure over the centuries, today it still basically maintains its original form. The huge cylindrical mass where the harmonic *Loggia di Bramante* stands out rises up on a squared base. A transformed fortress connected to the Vatican by a long, fortified corridor, it served as a refuge for the popes during sieges and popular uprisings.

A fountain in St. Peter's Square. This is the one on the left of the square, erected for reasons of symmetry about half a century after the one on the right was created by Maderno for Paul V to celebrate the arrival of the Paolo Aqueduct from Bracciano. This restored Trajan's original pipeline. The scales under the jets remind us of the Fountain of the Pinecone in the atrium of St. Peter's. (Today this is in a large niche in the Belvedere, in the Vatican courtyards.)

The Swiss Guard at the Bronze Gate. One of the last mercenary armies in the world is the handful of Swiss Guards that the Vatican retains to watch over the Papal palaces. The gesture is an expression of gratitude for those who gave their lives in St. Peter's Square, fighting against the Landsknechts who burst through Porta Cavalleggeri in 1527. The Gate leads to Bernini's royal staircase and is still the official entrance to the seat of the Papacy.

The Sistine room of the Vatican library. Sextus V, the great visionary of a Christian Rome, designed a gallery wing through the huge Belvedere courtyard to bring the books and archives forming the basis of ecclesiastical tradition and thought together in the heart of the papal residence. The room, which today houses temporary exhibitions, was decorated with lavish care.

The depiction of the *Original Sin and the Expulsion from Eden* in the Sistine vault is the dramatic highlight of this "people's Bible." An imaginary monumental architecture of pillars, architraves, dome vaults and lunettes divides up this space, in which figures of sculpted emphasis evoke prophets, sybils, and allegorical nudes to make up a framework for the story of the central panels.

Michelangelo's *Pietà* in St. Peter's. This work is "early" only in terms of the artist's age, as it is a consummate masterpiece. Anyone who has admired the heroic determination of the Moses and perhaps also knows the dramatic *Pietà's* of the artist's old age will have difficulty in imagining all of them being completed in the course of a single lifetime. Michelangelo Buonarroti was, however, a supreme artist precisely because of the breadth of experience, both personal and social, he embodied in his art.

The Last Judgement by Michelangelo in the Sistine Chapel. The immense fresco, painted 25 years after the vault, covers an entire wall of the Chapel. Ordered by Clement VII it is the pictorial representation of the *Dies Irae*. At the centre of the painting, Christ the Judge is surrounded by a multitude of chosen ones while a little lower, in St Bartholomew's tortured skin, the supreme artist left his self-portrait, almost as if taking part in the great event.

The *Laocoön* in the Vatican Museums. It belongs to the oldest part of these collections, which, unlike the galleries of antiquities and art in the courts of foreign capitals, did not constitute an integrated museum until the mid-18th century (the first Papal collection was assigned to the Capitol at the end of the 15th century). Integrated collections took shape under the impulse of the Enlightenment.

The canopy and the throne. In the projection of Michelangelo's vaults, supported by Bramante's pillars, lies the solemn area celebrating the primacy of the bishop of Rome. The canopy, which Bernini designed on the lines of the great Baroque scenic devices (the bronze comes from the girders of the Pantheon atrium), consecrates the Roman seat of the prince of the Apostles. The Papal throne is in the bronze composition in the background.

The vault of the Sistine Chapel, with Michelangelo's original colors recently restored, is a matchless artistic cycle that contributes significantly to Rome's uniqueness. With the panels of the lower fascia and the fresco of the *Last Judgement,* the famous Chapel is not only a high point of artistic creativity but also a sublime moment of contemplation of the eternal verities, of life and death, of good and evil.

The Gallery of the Chandeliers in the Vatican Museums. These rooms, created in the 19th century to house the collections, were designed to be magnificent, a worthy setting for the most august antiquities of Greece and Rome. The leading architects of the day took part in the work. The Vatican collections are some of the most famous in the world and attract a large number of visitors, many more than any of Rome's other museums.

Sunset over the Vatican and Janiculum hills, seen from the Trinità dei Monti promenade on the Pincio. The dome of the Vatican is framed in the cupolas, beacons, and bell towers of the twin churches of Piazza del Popolo, suggesting a stately ship rolling gently on the sea of the cityscape. In the depths of this turbid sea, the relics and artistic heritage of 30 centuries of human history lie hidden. This is Rome.

Photo Credits

All the photographs which appear in this book are by H. Simeone Huber except the following:

Via dei Fori Imperiali - I Buga Milan

Michelangelo, La Pietà - G. Cigolini
thanks to Archivio I.G.D.A. - Milan

The pictures of the Cappella Sistina frescoes and of the Last Judgement are by Takashi Okamura, © 1989 Nippon Television Network, Tokyo